The Christian Counselor's Commentary

Galatians
Ephesians
Colossians
Philemon

Jay E. Adams

MID-AMERICA
INSTITUTE FOR NOUTHETIC STUDIES

Institute for Nouthetic Studies, a ministry of Mid-America Baptist
Theological Seminary, 5640 Airline Road, Arlington, TN 38002
mabts.edu / nouthetic.org / INSBookstore.com

Galatians, Ephesians, Colossians, Philemon:
The Christian Counselor's Commentary
by Jay E. Adams
Copyright © 2025 by the Institute for Nouthetic Studies,
© 1994 by Jay E. Adams

ISBN: 978-1-949737-93-6 (Paper)
ISBN: 978-1-949737-94-3 (eBook)
Old ISBN: 0-9643556-2-0

Editor: Donn R. Arms

Library of Congress Cataloging-in-Publication Data
Names: Adams, Jay E., 1929-2020
Title: *Galatians, Ephesians, Colossians, Philemon:*
The Christian Counselor's Commentary
by Jay E. Adams
Description: Arlington, TN: Institute for Nouthetic Studies, 2025
Identifiers: ISBN 978-1-949737-93-6 (paper) | OCLC: 31960367
Classification: LCC BS2685.3 .A343 | DDC 225.7

Published in the United States of America

Introduction to
GALATIANS

In many other books of the New Testament we have seen how careful Paul is not to offend the reader. Indeed, as in II Corinthians, he often goes to great lengths to explain his words, his motives and his actions. Here, however, as every commentator points out, everything is different. In a passion of bare-knuckle writing, he takes the gloves off and sallies in for the knockout. No punches are pulled; Paul is infuriated.

Why? Not because the validity of his apostleship had been challenged, though it had. Not because personal innuendoes had been voiced about, though they had. No, the challenge leveled at him and his office was of importance only because it was one way that false teachers who had insinuated themselves into the Galatian churches could undermine his message. Yes, it was their challenge to *the message that he preached* that had so infuriated him. He had received that message of salvation by grace through faith directly from Christ Himself. It could not be in error. Yet, these Judaizing teachers were claiming that it was incomplete; OK so far as it went, but incomplete. They maintained that gentiles must first become Jews before they could become Christians. They must submit to the rite of circumcision and must faithfully keep the feast days of the Jewish calendar. Otherwise, they could not be saved. Paul (rightly) saw such teaching as a perversion—indeed, a repudiation—of the gospel. If the Galatians accepted this new teaching and taught it to others they would not only fall into serious heresy but would lead future "converts" to hell. It was a false gospel. That was the problem.

Paul's zeal for the purity of the gospel was driving him as he wrote. Forsaking the usual introduction to the letter, in which there is a more or less extended thanksgiving for the church to which he was writing, instead, Paul jumps into the fray with all four feet! Even the salutation, in which writers identify themselves and the recipients of the letter is an apologetic for the truth. Paul is not about to waste a line of papyrus with chitchat; he wants his readers *from the outset* to understand how serious the matter is. And both in content and in language, he reinforces the fact.

Who were these Galatians to whom Paul was writing? There are two views that I am not interested in discussing here. Let me simply say that I adhere to the North Galatian view. Are you Irish? Welsh? Scottish? French? Well, if your ancestry stems from any one of these, you are a Galatian. The names Gauls, Galatians and Celts all refer to the same people. In Asia Minor, Northwest of Tarsus, Paul's home town, was a settle-

1

ment of these people. Like many in their lineage they were emotional, lively and (sometimes) fickle people. How the gospel came to them is not recorded in the Book of Acts. But there is an extremely interesting reference in this letter to the fact that, in God's providence, Paul first preached the gospel to them because of problems he was having with his eyes. That is about all we can say concerning this matter.

Of what importance are these introductory facts to the counselor? Well, first, it is clear that there are times for him to engage in out-and-out warfare. While it is true of every aspect of the ministry of the Word (whether it be preaching or counseling) that you are always engaged in warfare, that warfare is not always carried on in the trenches. One is always struggling against principalities and powers as he ministers the Scriptures to others (see Ephesians 6:10 ff.). He is endeavoring not only to tear down walls men have erected to withstand the truth, in order to take their minds captive for Christ (II Corinthians 10:3ff), but he is also concerned that those who have surrendered to Him continue obediently in His service (II Corinthians 10:6). That was the problem here. The Galatians were quickly turning from the truth to error, a change that had been so rapid Paul himself was astounded.

Counselor, you may not like to do battle, but there are times when you must get down on the battlefield and grapple in hand-to-hand combat with the enemy. When your counselee is being fed some false, damning doctrine that seriously compromises the gospel, you cannot let that simply pass by. Paul didn't. In fact, in this letter, he is so strong that you probably would have a hard time emulating him. But, in spite of the emasculated training that many of you have had, there are times when you must stand for something. As Paul did, you may risk losing your counselees; but, regardless, you may not remain passive. You must tell it like it is. There are people on whom you, too, must cast an *anathema*.

Did Paul lose the Galatian churches to the Judaizers? There is no record that he did; but, then, there is no record that he didn't. The fact that the letter has been preserved, however, would seem to indicate that the congregation treasured it—even though it severely censured them—and for the benefit of other congregations, in humility and repentance, was willing to have it copied and distributed abroad. There is good reason, then, to believe that Paul's strong response had its intended effect.

But, whether the Galatians repented and drove the Judaizers away, or not, Paul had to do what he did—for the sake of the gospel. He had no choice. Nor do you. Recently, I found it necessary to condemn outright a congregation that a person was attending because, in it, they were teaching (among other errors) that one cannot be saved except by baptism by immersion, by their church. They claimed to be the only true church and said that people outside of it were lost. This had occasioned some confusion in the mind of the counselee who, some years previously, had trusted Jesus Christ as Savior and Lord. Had that message been incomplete? Did rites and ceremonies need to be added to the gospel? Of course not. I told her in no uncertain terms that 1) this church was heretical, 2) she should have nothing more to do with it and 3) that the teaching at that congregation was leading people to hell. While I did not use the word *anathema* that Paul uses in the first chapter, nevertheless, I had declared those who teach such things "anathema." In God's good grace she could see their errors as I opened the Scriptures and explained the truth to her. She has determined to attend a true church of Christ instead, even though it will be an inconvenience for her to do so.

You will not always win the counselee. You may be called narrow-minded, bigoted, etc., and your counselee may leave you. Paul (not to speak of Jesus) had experienced his share of such treatment too. It cannot be avoided. The truth of the gospel may not be compromised. It is likely that many counselors do enter into such compromise because they have been taught never to do the sort of things Paul clearly does in this letter. Whom will you follow? Paul? Or some Casper Milquetoast academic who never held (and couldn't hold) a pastorate, and who knows nothing to speak of about warfare in the cause of Christ?

So, then, we are about to embark on an expedition through the book of Galatians. Learn something, here, about how to be clear, sharp, pointed and concise in your language. Learn how to use arguments of all sorts (Paul will use eight in all) to prove your point. But, also, learn how to distinguish between those situations in which the defense of the gospel must be uppermost and when there is no such need (and, consequently, no need for sharp language).

When we come to the place in which Paul discusses the providential origin of the Galatian churches, having to due to his eye disease, we shall look more fully into seizing those possibilities that God's providence from time to time may afford alert counselors. This is an unexplored, but fruitful territory to traverse.

CHAPTER 1

> 1 Paul, an apostle, not sent from men nor by men, but by Jesus Christ and God the Father Who raised Him from the dead,

In the first five verses of Galatians Paul launches out immediately defending his apostleship, presenting the gospel and declaring the possibility and need to live holy lives in this godless age. Those three emphases constitute the three emphases of the Book. Chapters 1 and 2 explain why Paul must be considered a true apostle. Chapters 3 and 4 relentlessly present argument after argument to show that salvation is by grace through faith, rather than by Judaizing legalism. Chapters 5 and 6 show that grace, rather than legalism, leads to spiritual fruitfulness and newness of life.

It is important to establish the authority question first, straighten out theological or doctrinal issues that might become a source of trouble, and *then* move to the new behaviors that one must learn in order to live in ways pleasing to God. Though not always the direction to take in counseling, frequently, the same sequence may be followed with profit. If the counselee doubts your qualifications or proficiency, the authority question may be usefully pursued at an early point. This is true especially when, as in Paul's case, someone has *challenged* your ability or authority to counsel. Unlike Paul, you may have to appeal to the testimony of others when refuting claims against your ability. Sometimes such challenges are made by jealous or doctrinally antagonistic persons. Sometimes by psychotherapists who feel threatened by biblical counselors. Either way, for the sake of the counselee and the Name of Jesus Christ you must meet any challenge that indirectly tries to undermine biblical sufficiency by undermining you.

As for doctrine, you cannot avoid it. Every counselor, by virtue of the work he does, is a theologian who espouses and follows certain doctrines (I did not say all are *good* theologians). It may well be, in certain cases, that until a doctrinal issue is resolved, counseling can proceed no further. Every Christian counselor, therefore, should labor to become as doctrinally astute as possible. But, of course, if you do not know doctrine sufficiently, you will be inept to the extent that your doctrinal knowledge is insufficient. Every biblical counselor should have a well-worn copy of Berkhof's *Systematic Theology*.

As for the authority question, that may more easily be established. It is the Scriptures that lend authority to counseling. In the Bible God calls you to change the lives of others by means of the Bible (II Timothy 3:15-17). The authority by which you counsel is no less authoritative than that by which Paul preached; as for its basis, you too have a revelation from God—the Bible. I do not want to plow again ground that has already been plowed, disked and planted in my other books. For help, see *Competent to Counsel, The Christian Counselor's Manual, How to Help People Change,* etc. The biblical arguments have been set forth there in some depth.

As for the authority of others to counsel, you may turn the question around and ask where those who use the principles and methods of *men* derive their authority. This is a very legitimate question. And it is one they are hard-put to answer. Psychotherapists, marriage counselors, and others, who do not do biblical counseling as a mandate from God, are *self-appointed.* They have no authority other than the human authorities to which they do homage. It is very legitimate to ask who set them over others. After all, with the plethora of competing counseling systems out there—well over 250 in this country alone—who has the right to attempt to change anyone? Anyone, apart from a divine call and divinely-given revelation, who attempts to change the beliefs, attitudes and life-styles of others is either ignorant or arrogant. Either he knows little or nothing of the diversity of beliefs and practices in this field when he attempts to speak with authority or he arrogantly thinks he has adequately examined all other systems and is able to declare that he knows what (if anything) in them is right and wrong. The former stance reveals colossal ignorance of the field and the problematics within it, while the latter reveals a proud, self-assured arrogance. Persons of either sort are unfit to counsel. Which, in turn, means all who have no mandate from God counsel are without legitimate authority.

In verse 1, Paul identifies himself as the writer, who writes with the full authority of an **apostle**. He explains, as he goes, that this apostleship is of no secondary origin. An apostle is, literally, "one sent off." Paul makes it plain that he was sent off on his mission by God and not by men. His apostleship came through the Lord Jesus Christ Who, on the road to Damascus, confronted, converted and commissioned him (Acts 26:12-18). This could happen because, as he notes, Christ was raised from the dead. It was something extraordinary, though not impossible, then, for him to have a face-to-face encounter with Christ, the mark of a true apostle. Note the Source (God the Father) and the Channel (Jesus Christ) of Paul's apostleship were both divine.

2   and all the brothers who are with me, to the churches of Galatia:
3   May help and peace be yours from God our Fathers and from the Lord
Jesus Christ,
4   Who, in agreement with the will of our God and Father, gave Himself
for our sins to set us free from the present evil age,

But, while he is the writer, and while he received his commission
directly from Christ, he is no lone ranger. As he says in verse 2, the greeting comes not only from himself but also **from all the brothers who are
with me**. That means, among other things, that he was accepted by others
in the Christian church, he had their support in writing, and that his message was not some on the fringe, esoteric thing that only he and a few others held. He was in the mainstream of the church, as the "brothers" would
readily testify.

To identify with brothers from all over the church in your counseling
is also important. One thing that has characterized the nouthetic (or biblical) counseling movement has been its scriptural ecumenicity. Brothers
from all sorts of theological backgrounds, who believe in the Scriptures as
the rule of faith and practice, have been drawn to it. There is a universal-
ism to truth that eventually emerges. That has been forthcoming over the
last twenty-five years. While there is growing consensus within Christ's
church about the validity of biblical counseling, no other viewpoint has
gained such acceptance. In the church you will find various views from
outside that those who have adopted them have bootlegged into the
church. But none of these has commended itself to the church in such a
universal way as has biblical counseling. There is something to this that
from time to time you may wish to point out to doubtful counselees.

In verse 3, Paul wishes that they may know grace (help) and peace.
This is a part of his usual greeting. Certainly, those are not meaningless
words. What he wished was that they would come to know the peace (in
all the fullness of the Old Testament *shalom*) that those who are serving
Christ faithfully may have. And, he knew that they could not serve faithfully apart from the grace (continued assistance) the Spirit alone can give.
Surely, this troubled church needed both.

And so do your troubled counselees!

In verse 4, Paul says that Christ gave His life to save us from our sins
according to the will of God. This accords with his desire to see them
peaceful, availing themselves of the grace that He provides by the Spirit to
enable them to achieve *shalom*. After all, why shouldn't He? Didn't He

5   to Whom be glory forever and ever. Amen.

6 I'm, astounded that you are so quickly deserting the One Who called you by Christ's grace for a different "good news,"

---

send Jesus to die for our sins? If He did that, it is surely His will for us to have peace in our hearts as we draw upon His grace. And this comes as we, whom He has freed from the present evil age, live in accordance with that fact.

There is power for your counselee to live as God wishes. The same power that raised Christ from the dead, the same concern that brought Him to the cross in the first place, is the power and love available to live for His glory. When your counselee protests that the problems he is having stem from the world around in which he lives, you have, in this verse, an immediate answer: "You have been *freed* from the present evil age by the death of Jesus Christ. That means, of course, that there is no need to conform to it. There is no excuse for living sinfully. You have been set free! If you are not living freely, righteously, in accordance with God's Word, then, that is *your* problem; don't blame it on the world in which you live. You are in the world, but not of it." When he thinks of the remarkable fact that God has feed us from slavery to the world, Paul can only burst into a doxology in which he gives God glory (v. 5).

Now, it was just because the Judaizers were once again bringing Christians under law as the *means* of receiving salvation, peace and the ability to serve God, that Paul was concerned. He knew that it would not work. As he will show later on in the letter, the law was not given for such a purpose. It takes the grace of God to free one to live for Christ. He would not have them entangled in legal bondage.

Be careful, always, counselor, that you do not moralistically encourage counselees to conform to Scriptural commands *out of their own strength*. They will find themselves soon bogged down in failure, disappointment and despair. Point them in faith again and again to the grace of God mediated through the Word—with its promises and encouragements— by the Spirit Who enables them to understand and fulfill its commands.

Paul had seen it all. Not much took him by surprise. But he had to confess his amazement at the rapidity with which the Galatians (who shortly before were willing to give him their eyes for joy at hearing the gospel) were now deserting God. Don't miss the fact that Paul sees their desertion as a turning away from *God*, not from himself. Of course, they

7   which isn't really another; but there are some who are troubling you
and want to change the good news of Christ.

---

were deserting Paul; but to him that was not of importance. By giving
time of day to the message of the Judaizers, they were turning from God
Himself.

That is the note to keep sounding in counseling whenever a counselee, disagrees, attacks or attempts to vilify *you*. Remember, a counselee
may sling words at you that sting and are hard to bear, but, at bottom, he
or she is attacking God, not you. And, that is the note to sound in the
counselee's ears as well: you are not there to receive plaudits for what you
are doing; you are there to help the counselee deal with his problems with
God. All sin, ultimately, is a matter of the counselee's relationship to God.

The fickleness of people is something that every counselor must
learn early on. Today a counselee will praise you to the sky; tomorrow
you are dirt in his eyes. Today, he is willing to do whatever the Bible says;
tomorrow, he will disdain the very same teaching. But, don't give up. Paul
didn't. He weighed in and dealt with the problem of fickleness: "I am
astounded that you are so quickly deserting the One Who called you by
Christ's grace." Notice, too, that even in a statement of this sort, focusing
on the turning away that was beginning, he once more "puts in a plug" for
the true way of salvation: the One Who called them did so by Christ's
grace. They were called not through the works or ceremonies of the law,
but solely by the Grace of God in Christ! The words that Paul uses are calculated to say what he wants said—right from the beginning. Learn to
choose words carefully.

They were turning to "another gospel." Literally, this reads, "to a *different* gospel ('good news')". There are two distinct words used in the
original that in the KJ are translated by the one English word "another." In
verse 7, he explains that this new "gospel" is not another (of the same
kind; indeed it is not good news at all. If you said to your child "Honey,
go get me another diaper, the baby has soiled his," you would not mean
another just like the other! You'd want not another soiled one, but a clean
one. So, when Paul speaks of "another gospel" he uses the word from
which we get the first part of our word "*Hetero*sexual"—that is, one with
sexual desire toward another of a different sex. On the other hand, the
word used in verse 7, translated "another," means another *of the same
kind*. So, Paul is using the word "gospel" to refer to two very different
things: the true gospel and a *hetero*dox viewpoint that was no gospel at all

9

> 8 But even if we, or an angel from heaven, should announce "good news" to you that differs from the good news that we did announce, let him be cursed!

(even if the Judaizers referred to their teaching as such). Indeed, as he will have occasion to show at some length later on, the Judaizers were proclaiming a message that was the worst possible *bad* news.

When doctrinal error is this serious, you, like Paul, will find it necessary to distinguish truth from falsehood in equally clear terms. There are Christian counselors who will allow matters to ride, unwilling to make sharp distinctions. Don't be numbered among them. If it is the truth of God that changes people, then it is worth standing up for that truth whenever it is denied. No counselor can counsel biblically and effectively if he compromises God's truth.

Paul further explains: **there are some who are troubling you and want to change the good news of Christ**. The word for change, indicates a change for the worse. It means a perversion of the real thing. It has the idea of a reversal of what exists. And that is exactly what Judaizing was: it once more built up the very things that Paul had worked so hard to tear down. It was saying the opposite of the gospel: salvation is not by grace through faith, but by the merit of human works.

The word for "troubling" means to upset the solidity of what existed by causing factions or divisions. The churches of Galatia were being divided by these schismatics. Paul could not stand by and allow this to happen. He must speak out; strongly. And, he does. Today, certain radio and television gurus, self-appointed, unordained, who submit to no one other than themselves, pour their mixture of truth and error into the ears of Christians who tune into them day by day. Then, when they go to church on Sunday, and a man of God who has studied the Scriptures carefully tells them the opposite of what they have been hearing during the week, they attack him! It is a world like Paul's in which you live. Only the outward circumstances differ. The same basic difficulties prevail. That is why Paul's words and his approach are so important for you to understand and imitate.

In verses 8 and 9 the cannon blazes forth: Let them be *anathema!* Paul's strongest statement in any of his letters appears in these two verses. Not only does he say that persons who pervert the gospel should be cursed, but he says it *twice*. Not only does he say it twice, but to emphasize and strengthen his statement to the uttermost he even includes a

9   What we said before let me say again—if anyone announces to you a "good news" that differs from what you received, let him be cursed!

---

heretical angel! And, note well, it is not the doctrine on which he pronounces an anathema; it is on the persons who teach another gospel (which is not another of the kind he preached). Paul is saying, let them go to hell!.

The severity of this way of thinking and writing may be accounted for only on the basis that the preaching of a false gospel is so heinous, so damning to those who hear and believe it, that there is no other punishment severe enough to meet the crime. Paul was deeply concerned for the flock that was being attacked by the Judaizers. They were wolves among the sheep. Wolves must be destroyed. Paul's severity is born out of **love**, a fact hard for many today to understand. It is the fruit of a pastor's heart. He loved the Lord Jesus and His people so much that he would allow no one to distort the truth about Him to His people and stand idly by. Once before, when Stephen was stoned, he had stood giving willing consent. Never again, when Christ's church is attacked would he do so. This attack excelled that upon Stephen. In Stephen's case, his body was destroyed for a time (until the resurrection, when he would receive a new one); here the souls of men and women and children were likely to be destroyed eternally.

The word *anathema* was the Septuagint equivalent to the Old Testament word that meant "devoted to destruction." When Aachen hid some of the loot that had been acquired in battle, which God declared "devoted" (or anathema), it led to his destruction and that of others as well. To be devoted to destruction, as a New Testament curse, is to be devoted to destruction in hell for all eternity.

Strong sentiments. Strong language. Serious matters. That is what counselors and counselees alike must see when looking at this passage of Scripture. God is not playing games, giving us options as to how to be saved. He is not a foolish physician who says "take any medicine you like." There is one Savior and there is only one way: His. All other ways lead to destruction (Cf. Proverbs 14;12). There are certain nonnegotiables in Christianity. Counselees who try to "have it their way" and become upset with the counselor when he is unwilling to budge on those nonnegotiables, are like the novice using a computer. He says, "I thought this thing was supposed to be 'user friendly.' A friend will go half way with you. This computer, on the other hand, will not bend. Either I do things its way

> **10** Am I now trying to win man's approval or God's? Or am I seeking to please people? If I were still pleasing people I wouldn't be Christ's slave.

or it will not cooperate." Well, it *is* user friendly, if you are willing to submit to it. So too is God friendly to those who are willing to bend to His ways. But He will provide no second or third ways of salvation for those who prefer something other than what He has done in Christ. He stands by that once-for-all act. The same is true with all His commandments. When counselors, in harmony with the Word of God and its nonnegotiables, refuse to budge or bend, they are often labeled bigots. Doubtless, so was Paul. But that did not deter him from expressing a valid concern for the truth of the gospel. How sturdy are you in the face of undeserved hostile criticism? How much love for the Savior and His flock do you manifest in such situations?

We turn now to verse 10. Evidently, Paul had been accused of seeking human approval. He asks, "In the light of the statements I have just made (vv. 8,9), do you now think I am doing so?" At one time, before conversion, he was bent on pleasing people—the High priest, the members of the Sanhedrin, etc., but now, all that has changed. If he were still involved in the pursuit of approval from human beings, he would not be a servant of Christ. His servants live for only one word of approval: that "Well done, you good and faithful servant" of their Lord Himself.

Here is an area of great interest to the counselor. Approval by human beings drives many counselees. They are intimidated by others into commitments and actions that they don't want to make or do. They are afraid to do what they know the Lord wants them to do out of fear of what others will say. Explore this area thoroughly when counseling; especially whenever you find your counselee wanting to do the right thing, but reluctant to do it.

The problem is that the counselee's love for Christ is not as great as his love for himself. He does not want to be embarrassed, reprimanded, outcast, or to suffer whatever he imagines the consequences of biblical action might lead. He must be challenged about that. Love for Christ will grow, as one obeys Him *regardless of the consequences*. But that is where the problem lies: present consequences outweigh eternal ones. You must help your counselee to act not according to what these consequences may be (often they are quite different than he imagines) but according to biblical principles. Few factors loom as large in the counseling room as the influence of others who are not present. "What will my parents say? What

11 I want you to know, brothers, that the good news that was announced by me isn't according to human ideas,

---

will my unsaved husband do? How will I be able to face my friends?" These, and half a dozen other thoughts (often unspoken) may run through your counselee's mind as you try to guide him into biblical action. These are the unseen (and, as I have indicated, often unexpressed) roadblocks.

People who want the approval of others don't want to tell you that this is a problem for them because they think that, to do so, they will lose *your* approval. It is a vicious circle. Two things you can do to break into it: First, you can ask: "Are you afraid to do what God requires because of what someone might do or say?" But, if your counselee is caught in the dilemma of the vicious circle, *then* how do you break in? Put the pressure on: "God requires this. If you fail to do it, you will displease *Him*." Usually, as you are doing so, some statement will squeak out indicating the real problem is intimidation or fear of others. You can pick it up, turn it around for him to see all of its facets, and analyze it for what it is in his sight. Having come to grips with the truth, he must be brought to the right side of a choice—to serve God, seeking His approval—rather than to serve men and self for their approval.

Going on, we come to an extended passage (vv. 11-24) in which Paul defends his apostleship as a divinely-given office. Three things he affirms: He received his ministry from God, not from men. His former life as a Judaistic persecutor of Christians makes it abundantly clear that nothing less than a divine visitation would have changed him. And, his conduct, after conversion, is a clear indication of his independent commission from God. We need not develop every phrase and clause in this section, but there are certain facts that do stand out, that are of significance to the Christian counselor.

In verse 11, Paul makes it clear that what he preaches came from God and not from men. This, he says, is evident because the message itself isn't one that human beings could have originated. How would he, the Judaistic persecutor of Christianity, have devised the notion that the Christ he hated died for men's sins, and that no one can be saved by keeping the law, but only by faith in Christ? Where would he have gotten the notion that the gentiles (despised by pharisaical Jews) would be admitted to God's people, and, without first becoming Jews by circumcision and the keeping of the feasts? This is not a message that is in accord with human ideas, let alone the ideas that he had previously espoused.

12 because I didn't receive it from a human being, now was I taught it, but I received it as a revelation from Jesus Christ.

13 Now you have heard about my former pattern of life in Judaism, how I viciously persecuted God's church and tried to demolish it;

14 and how I advanced in Judaism beyond many of my contemporaries of my race, being an extreme fanatic for my ancestral traditions.

Frequently, as a biblical counselor, you will find yourself explaining to a counselee that what you are saying is not your idea, but God's. I have even heard myself say things like this: "If I were recommending a solution to your problem out of my own wisdom, I wouldn't suggest this one at all. But, it is *biblical*, and contrary to many of my own ideas, I know, therefore, it is the right thing to do." It may also be helpful at times when you are confronted with this sort of thing to show how others, dubious as the present counselee, followed the biblical admonition to the blessing of all involved. But, the person must never be encouraged to do what God requires merely because it works; he must do it because God requires it— to please and obey Him.

In verses 13 and 14, he recalls his former life. He was a vicious persecutor of Christ's church. Indeed, he went beyond all his contemporaries in this. He was fanatically attached to the oral traditions of Judaism (v. 14) rather than to the Scriptures. Interestingly enough, that is often the problem presented to the counselor. Tradition, custom, extra-biblical ideas and practices get in the way of biblical change. It is important to distinguish between the two; frequently, the counselee is unable to do so. He will have the two tightly intertwined. Your task in such cases is to do for him what God did for Paul: you must separate God's truth from the traditions of men. The two are not on an equal plain. Whenever a counselee views them as of equal authority, he finds that the traditions of men ultimately assume a place superior to the teachings of the Bible. That was what had happened in Paul's case. He, along with others in Judaism, studied assiduously what the Rabbis had to say rather than what God Himself said in His Word. And, as did Paul, they became fanatical for the traditions of the fathers. You will get nowhere in counseling until you have clearly established the Scriptures, rather than human traditions—even those of some church or group of Christians—as the basis for life and godliness. Often, simply making the distinction between the two authorities is all it takes.

Before he was born, God had planned to save and appoint Paul as an apostle to the gentiles. By grace, on the Damascus road, He called him

15 But when He who set me apart from before birth and called me through His grace was pleased
16 to reveal His Son to me so that I might announce the good news about Him to the Gentiles, my immediate response was not to confer with flesh and blood,
17 nor to go up to Jerusalem to those who were apostles before me; rather, I went away to Arabia and then returned again to Damascus.

---

into the faith and into that office (vv. 15,16). What did he do next? Check up on what God said by running the idea past the other apostles in Jerusalem? Absolutely not (vv. 16, 17). Instead he went away into Arabia, an isolated place all by himself.

When God speaks, one does not need a second opinion! Nor did Paul seek one. Fully assured of the basic truths of the gospel and of the task to which God had appointed him, he went away alone to sort things out. What would the effect of this revelation be on his thinking? For three years, he adjusted his thinking, probably searching the Scriptures in regard to the light which the newly-revealed gospel threw on them. Eventually, he went to Damascus, this time not as a persecutor, but as a preacher of the gospel.

Not only is it wise for a minister to spend three years in preparation for his ministry, as Paul did, but it is essential. And if you are a Christian already engaged in counseling who has never given adequate time to reflection on the Scriptures in relation to counseling theory and practice, then you probably need to set aside some time and do so. Many times new converts in counseling need the same advice. While they may never be called to a preaching or counseling ministry, they are called to live in "newness of life." Everything must change, business life, home life, etc., and they need time to reflect on just how the gospel will change their life-styles. A good counselor will be aware of this and urge new converts to examine not only the presentation problem(s), but their entire lives. That means he will branch out into areas in which the counselee was unaware of problems. While he cannot solve all problems in counseling, he can make the counselee conscious of the need to review all aspects of his life in the light of the gospel and at least get him started on the changes necessary in each.

Finally, Paul did go up to Jerusalem. This was not to confirm the truth of his message, but to meet Peter. He became acquainted with him and fellowshipped for fifteen days. The only other leader he saw was James. After that, he went to Syria and back toward his home in Cilicia.

18 Then, after three years, I did go up to Jerusalem to get acquainted with Cephas and stayed with him for fifteen days,
19 but I didn't see any of the other apostles except James, the Lord's brother.
20 (Now believe me, I tell you before God that what I write to you is no lie.)
21 Then I went into the regions of Syria and Cilicia.
22 But I wasn't known by sight to the churches of Judea that are in Christ;
23 all that they had heard was that "the one who used to persecute us is now announcing the good news of the faith that he once tried to demolish";
24 and they glorified God because of me.

During all those times he was not involved in instruction from others, but merely in getting acquainted with Peter and in pursuing his ministry. The churches of Judea didn't even know of him personally; they simply had heard that the one who persecuted has been converted and is preaching the gospel; and they glorified God for that.

There will be times when, in order to set to rest suspicions one counselee has concerning another, you will have to advise the one suspected to give a "blow by blow" description of exactly where he went and what he did, when. He may not enjoy doing this, complaining, "Well, she ought to trust me. She should take my word. Why should I have to go into details?" You may rightly point out that even the apostle Paul was not too proud to go into details with the Galatians for the sake of truth and good order. Surely if Paul could humble himself to this, your counselee can do so too.

All in all, the first chapter of Galatians is a powerful one, providing the counselor with much instruction and help. Spend some time thinking through additional implications of the things that Paul wrote. Indeed, it might be a useful policy to look for at least one more idea helpful to counseling in every chapter that we investigate together in this book.

CHAPTER 2

1 Then, fourteen years later, I went up to Jerusalem with Barnabas, taking Titus along too.

2 I went up in response to a revelation; and privately, before those who seemed to be the leaders, I openly explained the good news that I proclaim among the Gentiles, lest I run (or had run) the race for nothing.

As the second chapter opens, Paul is still defending his apostleship. Remember, he does this so vigorously, and at such length, because the gospel stands or falls with him as a revelatory person. Defending yourself as a true minister of Jesus Christ, since you are not one through divine revelation is given, is not as crucial. The revelation for which you stand is, however, and frequently, the counselee will (wrongly) identify what you teach with you as a person in such a way that, for him, both stand or fall together. While it was Paul's obligation to make such an identification, it is yours to deny it. You stand for the truth, but it, in no way, should stand or fall with you. Indeed, you, yourself, are totally subservient to it.

Paul now relates the reaction of the apostles when, long after he had begun preaching, he finally had an opportunity to discuss his message with them. Fourteen years after coming to Cilicia, he went up to Jerusalem with Barnabas and Titus. Probably Paul refers to a private conference in conjunction with the conference described in Acts 15. He went, not because he had a desire to check up on what he had been preaching—it would have been a little late for that! But because, in a revelation, God commanded him to do so. Here he openly explained the gospel he preached before the leaders of the church. After all, he didn't want his fourteen years or more of labor to have been in vain if they were going to send out people to tell his churches that his message was incomplete. The latter words in verse 2 do not express doubt about his own message, but doubt about how the leaders might react to it. The fact is, as he goes on to say, they added nothing to what he was preaching (v. 6).

When there is the possibility that the work you are doing in helping a counselee may be countermanded by another Christian, it is often necessary to confront that Christian to make sure that all you have done is not undone by him. Often, the person-to-person open explanation of the course that you have been following will elicit consent rather than disagreement. When it does not, you may find yourself in contention. But, it is wise to follow Paul's example here, at least for starters.

3 But even Titus, a Greek, who was with me, wasn't compelled to be circumcised;

4 not even on account of false brothers who had come in surreptitiously, who slipped in to spy on the freedom we have in Christ Jesus with the intention of enslaving us.

5 We didn't give in to them for a second to make sure that the truth of the good news might continue with you.

6 Now from those who seemed to be something (what they were really doesn't matter to me; God doesn't show partiality), nothing was added.

7 Indeed, on the contrary, when they saw that I had been entrusted with the good news for the uncircumcised, just as Peter had been for the circumcised

8 (He Who had worked in Peter to make him an apostle to the circumcised had worked in me also to make me an apostle to the Gentiles),

---

Further proof that there was no disagreement among the Jerusalem brothers with the message Paul proclaimed is found in the fact that Titus was not compelled to be circumcised (v. 3). They refused to make this a requirement for membership in the Christian church even though there were false brothers who slipped in surreptitiously who wanted to enslave gentiles and (evidently) insisted on this requirement. Paul combated them strongly, not giving in to their demands even for a minute (vv. 4,5). And, the apostles sided with him.

There will always be false teachers in the church, who demand that their ways be accepted. But you must not yield anything to them. They must be withstood. And, the apostles, who saw that the ministry to the gentiles and to the Jews had been given separately to Paul and Peter, gave Paul and his company the right hand of fellowship. By that action they acknowledged the divine commission given to Paul. It is good when brothers, finally having the opportunity to recognize one another's place in the gospel ministry, can shake on it. Though the nature of the Book of Galatians demands talk about withstanding error, it is also good to note those portions of it that speak of the unity of true saints.

It is too easy to become entirely combative, thinking there is no one else who has refused to bow the knee to Baal. The biblical counselor, who will find it necessary to combat error for the sake of God's Name and the welfare of his counselees, must, nevertheless, welcome joyfully all who stand with him. He must beware of making artificial and unnecessary divisions between himself and others. Some, in their zeal for truth, have done so. After all, as Paul observes, it was the same God Who was work-

9 and when they understood that grace had been given to me, James and Cephas and John, who seemed to be pillars, gave to me and Barnabas the right hand of fellowship, agreeing that we should go to the Gentiles and they to the circumcised.

10 There was only one thing that they urged—that we should remember the poor; and that is something that I have worked hard to do.

11 But when Cephas came to Antioch I opposed him to his face because he was obviously wrong.

12 Before certain persons came from James he ate with the Gentiles, but when they came, he withdrew and separated himself, fearing the circumcision party;

13 and the rest of the Jews acted hypocritically with him, so that as a result of their hypocrisy even Barnabas was led astray by them.

---

ing in both Peter and himself (v. 8).

The apostles *urged* (note, even this was not a command) Paul to remember the poor saints at Jerusalem. That is something, Paul says, he has worked hard to do. Certainly, while not requiring anything other of him in his preaching, it was not wrong for the leaders at Jerusalem to exhibit the dire need of their churches and to plead with Paul to help meet it. It is important to note that this is not a requirement, but, strictly speaking, it is a plea that has nothing to do with the preaching of the gospel itself. The request was not to be added to the gospel, but was to be a natural consequence, among those who believed, flowing out of gratitude for the good news by which they were saved.

There was, nevertheless, not that complete harmony of purpose and life that one would wish to see. Indeed, while there was no change in his doctrinal stance, Peter did compromise in practice in a way that might have given support to those who were preaching "another "gospel. As a result, Paul "**opposed him to his face**."

Why? Paul says, **he was obviously wrong** (v. 11). Before certain persons came from James he ate with gentiles, but after these Judaizers appeared, he, along with other Jews influenced by his example, withdrew and refused to eat with them. This was out of fear of the circumcision party (the Judaizers) which had developed in the church at Jerusalem. This hypocrisy even went so far as to include Barnabas (v. 13). Fear, along with a desire for approval, can be a powerful motive. Many counselees, even fine persons like Barnabas, go astray and act against their consciences out of fear. What did Paul do?

He opposed Peter to his face (note, he didn't go behind his back cut-

14 But when I saw that they weren't walking in line with the truth of the good news, I said to Cephas in front of everybody, "If you, who are a Jew, live like a Gentile and don't live like a Jew, how can you compel Gentiles to live like Jews?"
15 We, who by nature are Jews and not "Gentile sinners,"
16 know that a person isn't justified from works of the law but by faith in Christ Jesus. Even we believed in Christ Jesus in order to be justified from faith in Christ and not from works of the law; because nobody will be justified from works of law.

---

ting him down by slander). He did this in the presence of all (v. 14)—the other apostles, the Jews who withdrew and the Judaizers. He appealed to Peter's own example (v. 14) and once more explained the gospel message of free grace rather than works of the law (vv. 15,16).

It took boldness on Paul's part to do this. And, it will take boldness on yours when a great number of persons who know better are willing to compromise with false teaching in order to win favor and avoid confrontation. Like Paul, in meetings where erroneous ways are agreed to by word or example, you too may need to stand before all to expose the hypocrisy in the lives of those who, out of fear are willing to compromise. And, remember, it is not only by false teaching that error is propagated and truth accommodated, but also by bad example. Indeed, the latter may be even more powerful!

You may have to oppose others for the sake of your counselee. Others may be leading him astray by fearful, lax ways inconsistent with truth and with the biblical principles necessary to his improvement. If you do, it should be in the way that Paul did. Don't run others down behind their backs; be forthright: tell them to their faces. Prove them wrong in the presence of those involved. In this way, God's truth will prevail among all of them. We are not told the results here, but in the fifteenth chapter of Acts, it is clear that Peter and James and the rest agree with Paul. Evidently, this was a semiprivate, pre-council encounter. The results were salutary. If Paul had not stood for the truth in the face of all obstacles, humanly speaking, you today might not understand the way of life! Actions seemingly inconsequential, can have long-standing effects. Remember that. Let no one influence your counselee to compromise God's ways out of fear of consequences.

Having explained the gospel again (v. 16), setting faith over against works, Paul now continues to develop that message for the Galatians, who seem to have forgotten much that he taught them when he was with them.

17 But if while seeking to be justified in Christ we ourselves also were found to be sinners, is Christ then a servant of sin? Of course not!
18 After all, if I build again the same things that I have torn down, then I demonstrate that I myself am a transgressor.

In verse 17, he poses an intricate argument against the Judaizing error framed from the example of Peter. He asked Peter in front of the others that if he, while seeking justification through faith in Christ, is found a "sinner" (like the gentile sinners mentioned in v. 15 who needed justification), that is, if he is found to be a sinner under the law to which his example seems to indicate he has returned, then, does Christ's work do anything more than drive us back to condemnation? What better is it than the law itself? Jesus is not a Savior from sin if one is still a sinner in need of justification after believing the gospel. He is but a servant of sin, leading us into sin rather than into salvation.

Graciously, Paul uses the first person plural, including himself in the hypothetical conclusion that the doctrine of justification by faith leads only to further sin, when he is speaking of the example of Peter that seems to declare such a monstrosity. Having made one's point, pointedly, it is often wise to back off and speak hypothetically, even including yourself in what is said. This can help the counselee, or others who must be withstood, to hear whatever else you offer as an alternative to the false belief and behavior that you challenged.

Continuing his argument, Paul shows the foolishness of once again building up the law as a way of salvation when that is exactly what he has torn down. To do so, he would go back to being under its condemnation as its **transgressor** (v. 18). Through the law, which was his schoolmaster to bring him to Christ, he died to law. That is to say that he was no longer under its condemnation as a transgressor of it. His transgressions had been dealt with in the death of Jesus Christ on the cross.

Then, comes the great twentieth verse, sometimes misunderstood and misused to teach that there is nothing the believer can do to please God. Instead, he must let Christ do everything *for him instead of him.* But there is no quietism in the verse. When counselees from the higher life movement (so-called) tell you that is wrong for them to obey scriptural commands because then they (instead of Christ) would be doing what God commands, you must refute this erroneous notion outright. Otherwise, you will get nowhere in counseling. One way to do this is to ask the counselee to show you a single command given to Christ in you, or to the

19 I through law died to law so that I might live to God.

20 I have been crucified with Christ, and I no longer live but Christ lives in me. And the life I now live in the flesh I live by faith from God's Son Who loved me and gave Himself up for me.

21 I will not set aside God's grace; if justification comes by law, then Christ died for nothing.

Holy Spirit, that pertains to your behavior. He will not find it. Rather, if he begins the search, he will discover command after command given to *himself*. Well, then, what does the verse teach?

When Christ died, it was reckoned to you, believer, that you (instead of Him) were dying on the cross, bearing the punishment for your sins. He died in your place, bearing the wrath of God you deserved. In Christ, you died to your old ways. The old you (that old "I" mentioned here) no longer lives. The past is gone so far as the record goes. And the record also shows that Christ's righteousness is attributed to you as though you lived a perfect life. But, something more is true. Christ, in the person of the Holy Spirit, has taken up residence in you. Paul says He **lives in me**. That makes His illuminating and strengthening power available to you. And the life you (that is the new you) now live, you live by faith. And this faith is "from God's Son." It is a gift. It is He Who gives faith, increases faith, Who by means of His indwelling presence enables you to draw upon His truth in the Bible by faith in order to live for God as you should. The life you now live depends not upon keeping the law in your strength, but upon faith in Christ, Who alone enables you to do so.

While the higher life people are right in wanting to avoid doing things in one's own wisdom and strength, they have erred by calling on Christians to do nothing but "yield." They say "let go and let God." But they are wrong. Everywhere, the Bible calls on the Christian to obey. The biblical answer is found in neither extreme. Instead, you must call on your counselee to obey, not in his own wisdom or strength, but *in faith*, drawing on the wisdom of Scripture and the strength the Spirit supplies through this Book to do it.

I like verse 21, don't you? Paul, in a statement of faith and determination declares: "I will not set aside God's grace." It reminds me of Luther's great statement at the Diet of Worms: "Here I stand." There are some things about which you must be unmovable. If there are not, you are not fit to counsel. His conclusion is: if justification comes by means of keeping the law, then Christ died in vain. Surely that is true!

CHAPTER 3

1 Galatians, you are stupid! Who has put a spell on you, you before whose eyes Jesus Christ was placarded as the crucified One?
2   Tell me this one thing: did you receive the Spirit from works of law or from hearing with faith?

Having defended the gospel by defending his apostleship, Paul makes a direct appeal to the members of the Galatian churches to return to the simplicity of that gospel. This appeal takes the form of a series of arguments for justification by faith alone that grows naturally out of the transitional words found in 2:17-21.

Argument One: Personal experience. You ought to know better! That is the gist of what Paul is about to say. And, if you have knowledge of past experiences in the life of your counselee that relate to the point at which your counseling is floundering, that is not a bad approach (among others) at which to begin. If, for instance, your counselee claims that she cannot control her temper, but finds herself continually out of control, shouting at the children, like Paul, you too can say "Come on, now, you know that you are able to control yourself. Haven't you ever had an experience in which you found yourself screaming at the kids when the phone rings? What do you do? You pick it up and answer—but you don't scream, do you? You say, "Yes? Oh, hello Mrs. Neighborhood gossip. Why no, you didn't disturb me at all. I was just talking to the children, etc, etc..." What did you do? You *controlled yourself.* You can do so when you want to. You can do so when you think it might embarrass you not to. You don't do so when you think you can get away with it. That is all there is to it. You care more about what Mrs. Gossip would say all over the neighborhood if she would hear you shouting at the top of your lungs than what it does to your children. Obviously, your values are misplaced, you need to repent, and start controlling yourself in front of your children just as you did when the phone rang!

At any rate, Paul reminds them of what they already knew: their lives had been changed by the work of the Spirit through God's grace, and not by the works of the law. No wonder he begins the argument with the words **Galatians, you are stupid!** Those words should not be softened any more than the words in Chapter one when Paul fires an anathema at those teaching a false way of salvation. Paul is out to awaken the Galatians; because they *needed* it. "It is as if you have been fascinated, spell-

> 3   Are you really so stupid? Having begun by the Spirit are you now going to be completed by the flesh?

---

bound by these false teachers, so that you fail to see the obvious. How could we have made the message any clearer?" he asks. "After all, we etched it out so clearly it was as if we **placarded** Jesus Christ crucified before your eyes. We made the simple gospel plain as can be." It was like putting the message on a roadside billboard!

But, what was true of the Galatians is often true of your counselees as well. They may become so fascinated with the teachings, vocabulary and jargon of the psychotherapeutic community that they forget the very simple truth that it was Jesus Christ who got them out of the most difficult problem that they will ever face; He freed them from the curse, penalty and dominion of *sin*. If He could do that, is it wise to turn to the teachings and procedures of men as the answer to personal problems of a much lesser magnitude? No, that is as stupid as the turning of the Galatians to Judaizing legalism!

Paul presses the issue in v. 2: "Tell me this one thing only," he commands, thus emphasizing the point, How did you get the Spirit? Was it through attempting to fulfill the law? Was it through your good works? Or was it from hearing the gospel—the true one—in faith? They, of course, knew the answer to that one: they received the Spirit, with all of the obvious manifestations of His work that accompanied His reception under apostolic preaching (v. 5) by faith in the gospel alone. It was an undeniable fact. Works, ceremonies like circumcision, neither brought about that result, nor were they necessary for it. So, too, the question comes today, how does one receive the Spirit? Not by works of righteousness he attempts to do, but, again, by the hearing of faith (that is, the hearing of the gospel message blended with faith in the hearer). Although miraculous works no longer accompany His coming into the lives of those He saves, the lifting of the crushing load of guilt and the subsequent transformation of those lives is clear evidence of the Spirit's presence. So, asks Paul, are you going to begin one way, but abandon that to be **completed** in another (v. 3)? It is a good question. Especially for those who want to follow a two track way of finding help from counseling.

What do I mean by that? Simply this. Many will follow Christian counsel for *some* aspects of their problems, but will turn to secular counsel for others. That will not do. If you are wise, you will, for instance, tell counselees (as I recently told two) that they must *choose* between Christian counseling and other counseling they were receiving. Happily, both chose Christian counseling. One, on his own, had decided to make that decision, before I mentioned it. He told me, "What you said and what she (the other, non-Christian counselor) said were exactly the opposite. So I knew that I had to make a choice." That is always true when it comes to God's truth. God requires complete, never partial, adherence to His ways. You cannot straddle the fence. You can't root for both teams. As Paul made clear to the Galatians, when you do so, it is two different ways that you are trying to go—actually, opposite ones! Why would you abandon one that has already proven a blessing to you for one that has not?

Again he asks, "Are you so stupid?" implying, "I surely don't think you *could* be." When Paul says something twice (as he did in chapter one when anathematizing the false teachers) we must recognize he does this for the purpose of strongly emphasizing it. Counselees who want to keep one foot in each camp are stupid and, so, likewise must be faced with the decision to abandon other ways of sanctification proposed by cultists, false teachers, and psychotherapists. As Paul will show later on, the works of the flesh do not produce the fruit of the Spirit; indeed, they produce just the opposite. Much counseling fails because people want to hedge their bets; you can't do that with God. He will not share His counseling load with Freud! You will never find Him doing such team counseling. And, remember, ultimately, even *you* are not the counselor, the One Who actually effects counseling changes is the Holy Spirit. All you and I may do is minister the Word that He uses to effect the desired growth out of sin into righteousness. Neither you nor I ever changed anyone (at least for his good!). It was always the Spirit working through His Word. Put it to the counselee: what do you want, anyway, the Spirit or some man to change you? The Spirit works in the context of His Word; He makes no promise to work in any other. It is, therefore, nothing short of stupidity to remove one's self from that context to another.

Pushing the point further: you suffered for the gospel. We don't know what they suffered or how; Paul does not elaborate. Minimally, at least, it must have been jeering, ostracism. Some, in those days, of course, suffered torture and even death. But, Paul asks, was the suffering for nothing? "Of course not," is the answer that rhetorical question requires. "Well, then, remember how you believed it important enough to boldly

5 (if indeed in vain)? Does, then, the One Who gives you the Spirit for support and Who works miracles among you do it from works of law or from hearing with faith?

---

defend the gospel? Why, now, are you departing from it for some novelty which is not new at all, but which has blinded you to all of this?

That is how Paul extended the argument from experience. Actually, there was nothing new about this supposed way of salvation by doing **works of the law**. The Jews had been trying it for years—and had failed. God will not accept man's faulty attempts at self-salvation. The law cannot save anyone. He will go on to show, later on, that the law serves only to point guilty sinners to Jesus Christ, Who alone can save through His death and resurrection.

The Galatians were fascinated, entranced, spellbound by the rhetoric and persuasiveness of the Judaizers, so that they could no longer perceive simple, obvious truths. So, too may your counselees be. The arguments given, "all truth is God's truth," and "there is, you know, such a thing as general revelation," etc. by integrationists, combined with the array of technical terms that they love to use, tend to fascinate and, thereby, move one from the simple teachings of Scripture. "Scripture is OK so far as it goes," they argue, "but it does not go far enough. You need something more." That was precisely the argument used by the Judaizers: "Paul's message is incomplete. There is more that we can add to it." Always beware of the "something more" approach. It is often no different, in the long run, from the "something different" one. Both challenges to God's Word are serious. Indeed, from the garden, that has always been the devil's tactic: question the accuracy or the adequacy of God's Word.

That is Paul's first argument: Look at your own experience. Of course, if the Christian thinks it through, he will have to admit that whenever he was willing to trust God's Word wholeheartedly for what it says, adding nothing to it, it never failed. That is your counselee's "experience" with God to which you may point. However, note the qualifications in the above sentence: "wholeheartedly," "adding nothing" and "for what it says." Many have had bad experiences with the Scriptures because they failed in one or more of these respects. They either trusted partially (perhaps doubting or trusting in something else as well) or they trusted the wrong thing thinking that was what the Bible teaches. In such cases, if counselees protest that the simple trust that you are advocating failed, you must lead them back through the ways they went to expose the errors that

6 It is just as it was for Abraham, who **Believed God and it was reckoned to him for righteousness.**

7   You must understand, then, that it is people with faith who are the sons of Abraham.

8   The Scripture, foreseeing that God would justify the Gentiles by faith, announced the good news beforehand to Abraham: **In you all the Gentiles will be blessed.**

---

they thought (wrongly) were God's ways. As Isaiah 55 makes clear, man has a tendency to think his ways are God's ways, when they are not. God's promises do not fail!

Argument Two: The Case of Abraham. This argument runs from verses 6-14. It is powerful and important for many reasons. Paul sets forth the pith of his argument at the outset: Abraham **believed God and it was reckoned to him for righteousness**. The implications of that simple, but profound, fact are worked out during the remainder of the section. What are they? Well, first, Paul says, "people with faith are the sons of Abraham" {v. 7). "These Judaizers want you to become Jews, do they? So, let us ask who are true Jews? They are the sons of Abraham, aren't they? Of course they are. How do you become a Jew? The way Abraham did. But, if you want to be like Abraham, you must be saved as he was. How was Abraham saved? By faith. That is what the passage of Scripture I just quoted teaches. You must be justified by believing—just as Abraham was. To become his sons (that is, to be like him) you too must believe, just as I have been saying all along."

Moreover, Scripture teaches that **in him** all the gentiles would be blessed (v. 8). How does that happen? Just as the Old Testament prophecies foretold: God had determined to justify the gentiles **by faith**. The gospel, consequently, was announced beforehand to Abraham. In other words, Paul was saying, "These Judaizers want you to become Jews in order to become Christians. Well and good. You do become Jews when you become Christians; it is Christians, those who believe in Jesus as the Messiah, who are justified (declared righteous) by faith. Jew and gentile alike must come to God through Jesus; it is by faith, and faith alone that people become sons of Abraham—they are justified just exactly the way Abraham was, long before the law was given. And, this is nothing new: as the Scriptures indicate in the promise to Abraham, in Him all the gentiles (nations) will be blessed.

So, concludes Paul, people with faith are blessed with Abraham who had faith (v. 9).

9   So then, people with faith are blessed with Abraham who had faith.

10 Now, all who depend on works of law are under a curse; indeed, it is written, **Cursed be everyone who does not continue to do all those things that are written in the Book of the Law.**

Paul's argument is tight. It is Scriptural. It is devastating. He has turned the Judaizers' own guns upon them. They were requiring people to become Jews in order to become Christians. Paul shows that it is precisely what he is preaching: gentiles must become Jews (sons of Abraham) by faith. Hebrew is an ethnic term; Jew is a religious one. Sometimes people get that mixed up. The preferred way of speaking, perhaps, is to speak, as Paul does, of those who are the "sons of Abraham."

Now one can see how important it is to know the Bible. In counseling, you will have to meet many seemingly biblical arguments that are addressed to you by your counselees. Either they will repeat what others have told them, or they will express wrong ideas and interpretations of passages that they, themselves, have accepted. As Paul does, it is often necessary to show them what the Scriptures really teach about matters under discussion. Suppose, in a counseling session, a counselee tells you, "There is probably no hope for me since I am one of those adopted persons who will receive the judgment of the fathers that passes down to the third and fourth generation." What would you say? Knowing the Scriptures, and aware of the fact that there have been teachers (one in particular) who have spread such unbiblical teaching abroad in Bible-believing circles, you would be ready with your answer. "But, my friend," you might reply, "You have quoted only part of the verse" (a problem with the teacher I have mentioned), "it continues, 'of them that hate me.' Do you hate God?" "Well, no, of course not," he might respond. "Well, then," you continue, "the verse, qualified as it is, doesn't apply to you, does it?" "I guess not," he may say. "And," you continue," there is still more: God promises to "show mercy" to "thousands" of generations of "those who love Me and keep My commandments." There is a positive promise to which you may also relate."

How important it is to know what the Scriptures truly teach! Then, and only then, you can refute the foolish and erroneous notions that people get in their heads (or are taught) that have a lot to do with the problems they present to you as a counselor.

Let's take another example. A counselee is not sure that he is saved. He has read the King James version of Romans 8:16 in which we are

11   That nobody is justified before God by law is clear because **the just person lives because of faith.**

12   The law does not require faith, but rather: **Whoever does these things shall live by them.**

---

taught the great truth that the Spirit testifies (or bears witness) "with our spirit" that we are the children of God. He says, "I must not be a child of God because, even though I think I am from time to time, I have never heard or felt any witness to the fact from the Spirit." He is waiting for something that will never happen. It will not because the verse does not teach what he thinks it says. There is no promise that the Spirit will communicate directly with him in some way, telling him that he is a child of God. If he had a copy of *The Christian Counselor's New Testament* he would understand the verse quite differently. There, it reads, "The Spirit Himself testifies together with our spirit that we are God's children." The "with," as he had been reading it, meant "to." But that is not what the original Greek says at all. The Greek word is *sun*, a preposition that means "together with." It cannot mean "to." What the verse is saying is that, according to the requirements of the law, there is more than one witness to the fact of your salvation. You possess an internal assurance, but the Spirit—in the Bible—also (indirectly) testifies to your salvation if you have faith in Christ. So, there are two witnesses to the fact.

But, getting back to Galatians 3:10ff. Paul now shows the Galatians that the Judaizers are misusing the Scriptures in another way: they erroneously teach that one must keep the law to be saved. Paul observes that this is a very serious departure from truth, with serious consequences. Referring once more to the Scriptures, which he properly applies, he observes that **all who depend on works of law are under a curse**. Then, backing up his point, he quotes Deuteronomy 27:26 (v. 10), and goes on to say "That nobody is justified before God by law is clear," also quoting Habakkuk 2:4, "The just person lives because of faith." The passage means, that he, who being justified by faith, shall live. The just person, here, is the one who is righteous, or justified, by faith and thus lives (has life that is truly life), here, and throughout eternity.

And, as he says, placing one's self under the law *as a means of salvation* is to abandon faith altogether (v. 12), since the law does not require faith, but obedience (here he quotes Leviticus 18:5). So, if the Galatians follow the teachings of the Judaizers, instead of the teaching of Paul, they have placed themselves under a curse. That is serious. Because, the law

13 Christ redeemed us from the curse of the law, by becoming a curse for us (it is written, **Cursed is everyone who hangs on a tree**),

14 so that by Christ Jesus Abraham's blessing might be realized by the Gentiles, and that through faith we might receive the promised Spirit.

---

demands perfection, and no one will achieve it. All who try keeping the law for salvation will be cursed under the divine wrath (the word for curse in these verses is not the *anathema* we encountered in Chapter one, but one that means an expressed declaration of God's consuming wrath). "However unwittingly, these men to whom you are turning are not your benefactors, they are bringing you under a curse," Paul is saying. In other words, those who trust in their supposed "gospel" will find, in the long run, that far from preaching "good news," their doctrines lead only to hell.

When a counselee is suffering because of faulty teaching, is confused or ensnared in cultic or non-Christian teaching, it is essential to take time to refute the error. Truth blesses, now and later on. Error harms, now and in the future as well. Because of this fact, if you really want to help the counselee, you will be prepared to discuss doctrinal issues whenever they are essential to the counselee's welfare. It is, of course, impossible to deal with all error in any counselee. Paul does not attempt to do that either. He focuses on the one issue that is damning, and therefore harmful to the reader and dishonoring to God. You will want to be sure, before bringing up doctrinal matters for intensive discussion, that those you raise bear on the difficulties the counselee is experiencing. Otherwise, you could get bogged down in all sorts of things that would, eventually, by prolonging sessions, be counterproductive.

"But," you protest, "does that mean I should allow all sorts of aberrant doctrine to creep into counseling sessions?" No, of course not. You will continue to operate according to those teachings that you hold as you counsel, not hesitating to refer to them whenever it becomes necessary to do so. Incidentally, frequently you will find yourself teaching more biblical doctrine that way than engaging in a discussion of these doctrines with the counselee. No one expects you to abandon your beliefs or to counsel in any other way than in accordance with them. My concern is simply that you not make an issue of any doctrinal difference unless it is essential to do so. Naturally, we are talking about those beliefs that you hold which have been derived from the Scriptures by careful exegesis. It would never be proper for you to introduce speculations or loosely-held views into counseling. You represent yourself as a Christian counselor who will

15 Brothers, let me illustrate this by an example from human relation-ships; nobody sets aside or adds to a human covenant once it has been rati-fied.

16 Now, the promises were said to pertain to Abraham and to his Seed. If doesn't say, "and to his seeds," as though it were speaking of many, but says rather, speaking about One, "and to your Seed," Who is Christ.

---

counsel in strict accordance with the Bible.

Verse 13 is the crux of the matter. We were all under the law's curse by the covenant of works made with Adam in the garden, but Jesus Christ has redeemed us from this curse. We must not return to that from which Christ has freed us. To do so is not only retrogression into a damning legalism, but also a calumny cast upon the work of Jesus Christ. He, according to the Bible, hung on the tree, being cursed in our stead. He took the curse of the broken law upon Himself when he died for our sins. And, as a result of His work the blessing promised to Abraham is now being realized among the gentiles: they are receiving the promised Spirit.

Notice how the promise of the Spirit is equated throughout this book with the blessing to the gentiles given to Abraham. This is understandable since in Joel 2:28 and Ezekiel 36:27 this prediction is clear. The surpris-ing thing to Peter and those all around was that the Holy Spirit fell on the gentiles just as, at Pentecost, He was poured out on the Jews (c. Acts 10:44-47). And this also was the determining factor in Peter's report (Acts 11:215-18), that which led the group to quiet down and accept gentiles into the church. And, finally, it was the clincher at the Jerusalem confer-ence (Cf. Acts 15: 8-12). The coming of the Holy Spirit upon the gentiles, then, was the vital sign that the Old Testament promise to Abraham had at long last been fulfilled. That is how Paul can so closely identify the two.

Argument Three: *The example of a covenant.* Actually, this argu-ment, beginning in verse 15 piggybacks on the case of Abraham, but is essentially a separate argument altogether. Paul offers an "example" from what everyone knows about human relationships: he says, "nobody sets aside or adds to a human covenant once it has been ratified." Once the agreement has received its official status, it remains *as is.* Apply this fact that we all acknowledge to the covenant with Abraham (v. 16). This cove-nant pertained to Abraham and to His Seed. That one seed is Christ. The promise of blessing the gentiles was made to Abraham and to Christ. (See in-depth commentators for a discussion of the singular and plural matter.)

Proceeding with the argument, Paul next points out that the law,

31

17 Now this is what I am trying to say: the law, that came 430 years afterward, doesn't annul a covenant that was previously ratified by God, so as to invalidate the promise.
18 If the inheritance is from law, it is no longer from promise; but God gave it to Abraham by promise.

---

coming 430 years after the Abrahamic covenant, in no way annulled that covenant because it was ratified by God. The promise of salvation by faith—to Jew and to gentile alike—persisted. It continued, as did the covenant, alongside the law as the way of salvation, and now had received its complete fulfillment in the ingathering of the gentiles as sons of Abraham by faith. The coming of the law did not invalidate the promise.

Use of good examples in counseling is altogether necessary. Paul is writing to people, people who (at bottom) are no different from you or your counselees. Everyone resonates to a story or example that, simply put, illustrates a point that might otherwise remain foggy. Illustrations, as the word itself means, throw light on something. Use them freely *for that purpose*. Illustrations used in preaching or in counseling simply for relief are odious; illustrations that concretize or clarify what is being said are valuable. A counselor with a fruitful mind will be able to shake illustrations out of his sleeve at a moment's notice. Most will have to begin to compile illustrations to be used during counseling sessions. One way to begin to work on this matter is to acquire a notebook into which you regularly, every day, write at least three, illustrating some counseling point. It doesn't matter how good they are at first. As you continue, you will get better. And, as you go back over some of the earlier examples (shudder!) you may find that the germ of a good example lies dormant in it and with a little additional effort it can be brought into a useful shape.

It is probable that Paul used the example of a human covenant before—or, if this was the first time he employed it, he probably used it again and again in a variety of contexts in which he found it useful. Examples may be used more than once, sometimes necessarily adapted to the specifics of a situation, but, nevertheless, useful again and again. Begin to build a repertoire of them.

The inheritance of the land, Paul goes on to say, was not from law, but from promise (v. 18). He has made his point. In no way is anything that Abraham received from the law; there was no such law in Abraham's day. Abraham believed God and by his faith received all the promises. That covenant, that made the Hebrews sons of Abraham, now makes

19 Why give the law then? It was added be cause of transgressions until the Seed to Whom the promise had been made would come; and it was enacted through angels by the hand of a mediator.

20 Now a mediator isn't needed when there is only one party; but God is one.

21 So then, is the law contrary to God's promises? Of course not! The fact is that if a law had been given that could give life, then surely justification would have been by law.

---

believing gentiles (as God had promised) Abraham's sons as well.

Argument Four: The purpose of the law. If the law cannot save, why give the law? Paul asks the question that must have been in the mind of the reader (v. 19). The question was a natural one growing out of the previous discussion. But the answer to it also further proves Paul's contention. It is a good way to move, taking up one thing after another as they naturally develop from matters previously discussed. Paul says the law had a temporary function. It was added to the Abrahamic covenant (note: the covenant is still in force alongside of the law) until—but only until—Christ should come. And, it was added **because of transgressions**. What does that mean?

It means that God wanted to make it perfectly clear what His will is and that when it was not fulfilled either by acts of commission or omission everyone would know that he had transgressed. The law was to make transgressions known. Where there is no sign, one might protest that he did not know that it was against the law to fish in the pond. On the other hand, the fellow leaning up against the very tree on which a "No fishing" or "No trespassing" sign is posted knows perfectly well that he has broken the law. That is the purpose the law served.

Again, the law was given to Israel by means of a mediator. Moses stood between God and man as the mediator to whom the law was directly given. Israel, then, received it indirectly. A go-between (mediator) implies not one, but two parties to the transaction, in this instance, one of Whom was God. But, in contrast, Abraham received the promise about the gentiles *directly*. There was no mediator on that occasion.

Well, the reader might have thought, Paul is against the law. Not so. It in no way contradicts God's promises (v. 21). Indeed, it is so fine that if there ever had been a law that could have provided life (salvation) then this one is it. Nevertheless, justification was not in view as the purpose of the law when it was given. There was no need for that; the matter had been clearly set forth to Abraham long before: faith was counted for righ-

22 But the Scripture locks up everybody under sin so that the promise that is realized by faith in Jesus Christ might be given to those who believe.

23 Now before the faith came, we were guarded under law, being locked up for the faith that was going to be revealed.

24 So the law became our guardian until Christ came, that we might be justified by faith.

25 But now that the faith has come we are no longer under a guardian.

26 You are all God's sons through faith in Christ Jesus,

---

teousness. What the law did was to lock up everyone (so that no one could escape). None could escape its condemnation as a sinner. That was so that those who recognized and confessed their guilt and trusted in the coming Messiah might receive the promise (v. 22). Thus, the law had a gracious purpose: to drive men to Christ for justification.

Now, prior to the coming of the faith (note the article, which here means the Christian faith with its beliefs), we were all kept under lock and key by the law. That is to say, until Christ actually came and died and the gospel was a reality, the law condemned and people looked forward by faith to His coming, but the "revealed" reality had not yet appeared. All the law offered was types and shadows. So, the law became a guardian until Christ came. Now that He has appeared and died and risen, there is no longer any need of coming under a guardian. The death of Christ, far more vividly portrays the sins and iniquities of man than the law could ever do. That the Son of God had to die for guilty sinners shows the wretched heinousness of it all.

The "guardian" here is *pedagog*, a term referring to the slave that made sure the schoolboy got to school and worked hard while he was there. It is an image Paul will enlarge upon later on.

But now, we have all grown up and are sons, not simply children under a trainer, through faith in Christ Jesus (v. 26). There is a closer, clearer unity with God in this New Covenant than there was under the law. All those who have been truly baptized into Christ, have been clothed with Him. Baptism, in the New Covenant era, means union with Christ and His church. Those who are united (the meaning of *baptizo* is not "immerse," but "merse." In good English, that is changed to "merge." That is why one is said to have "put on" Christ when the Holy Spirit baptizes him into Christ) to him no longer need a *pedagog*.

And, concludes Paul, it doesn't matter whether you are a Jew or Greek, a slave or free person, a male or a female, there are no longer any such distinctions with reference to Christ's church: you are all united in

27   since as many of you as were baptized into Christ have put on Christ.

28   There is neither Jew nor Greek, there is neither slave nor free, there is neither male nor female; you are all one in Christ Jesus.

29   And if you are of Christ, then you are Abraham's seed, heirs in keeping with the promise.

Him. If all have "put on" Christ, and are, therefore "in Christ," all are the same in Him. And all who belong to Him are Abraham's seed (the further extension of the promised seed is to all who are in Christ), and, therefore, heirs according to the promise.

The argument is somewhat intricate, but when followed, powerful. Since all are joined together in Christ, all are viewed the same way. There are to be no distinctions about the way of salvation; it is the same for all.

Well, what has all of this to do with counseling? Not a great deal, directly. But, remember, we are interested in two things: content and methodology in dealing with people. One thing that can be said is that Paul expected his readers to use their brains when he wrote to them. Counselors may expect the same. Everything does not have to be made equally simple. Some things, by their very nature, are more intricate or complex than others. When set forth clearly, that is all that the counselee should expect. Some counselors insult their counselees by talking down to them. They act as if they were still the little children who need to be minded by the *pedagog* (of course that may be true of some)! But, the average Christian needs to be stretched in his understanding of the ways of God with men. That is possibly one of his problems: he may never have been challenged with any of the harder truths of the faith. He may have always been sucking the milk of the Word from his bottle. Babies, sucking bottles are cute; adults doing the same are not! When a meaty truth is the answer to a counselee's problem, explain it to him. Help him to grow not only out of his problems but also into a greater knowledge and love for the Scriptures. Notice how all through this chapter Paul opens up the Scriptures to these Galatians. That's the way to deal with confused Christians. Don't merely repeat what they already know, give them fresh insight into the truth of the Word.

Notice, moreover, the absolute authority with which Paul uses Scripture. What the Bible says is final; that's it. He doesn't have to justify statements from the Old Testament. What he must do is explain and apply them. Your task is the same. When you counsel Christians (and, remember, you should only counsel believers), you can expect them to accept the

Bible as the Standard for faith and life. There is no need to justify doing so. That is the premise on which counseling begins. Persons who want to counsel on some other premise, do not want Christian counseling. Be sure that you strongly assert this position by the way in which you refer to the Bible as the final Word. After all, it is!

CHAPTER 4

1 What I am trying to say is that as long as the heir is a minor he is no different from a slave even though he is the owner of everything.

2 But he is under guardians and stewards until the time that was set before hand by his father.

3 So too we, when we were minors, were enslaved by worldly elements.

Argument Five: The Minor and the Mature. Paul continues the comparison and contrast between a slave and a minor son. So long as he is a minor, the son, he observes, is no different from a slave—even though he is the heir to everything. This is a somber thought. A minor child, in those days, was not accorded all the rights of children in our country today; they were strictly subject to the authority of their parents. While there is no need to expostulate on the advantages and disadvantages of the two systems, there is no doubt that because of this, in many respects, Paul's comparison would no longer hold true.

What, in particular, does Paul wish to point out? In verse two, he mentions how the heir, as a minor, is under the care of guardians and stewards, and that this state of affairs will continue until the time that his father set for releasing him from this "bondage." So, in like manner, Paul points out, before coming to Christ, we too were enslaved to the world's "elements." The world's elements is a peculiar expression. It is difficult to understand its exact referent. It sometimes means the "ABC's" while at other times refers to the basic elements of something or other (even presuppositions). And, there is a more remote reference to supposed heavenly beings. Here, it seems that it refers to those elemental things understood by a child when still in his minority. The simple first teachings that one learns early in life. When still under Judaism or paganism, it was like living as a child; the law did not recognize those who were under it as mature, and the basic elements of pagan thought and life only enslaved to sin.

It is possible, however, that Paul is contrasting physical with spiritual religion, as when, in Hebrews 9:1, physical worship in a physical temple is referred to as a "worldly temple." Worldly elements, understood thus, would mean worship that was material, physical rather than that which is spiritual (cf. Jn. 4:21-24).

Whatever one may say about these verses, they do make it clear that in biblical times, it was understood that clear relationships were retained

> 4 But when the time had fully come, God sent forth His Son, born of a woman, born under law,
> 5 to redeem those who were under law so that we might receive adoption as sons.
> 6 Because you are sons, God sent forth the Spirit of His Son into your hearts, Who calls out, "Abba" (that is, "Father").
> 7 So through God you no longer are a slave, but a son; and if a son, an heir as well.

between the parent, who wielded authority, and the child who submitted to it. Something of that certainly needs to be communicated to youngsters who, in our time, seem to respect little or no authority over them. In counseling, one must, therefore, maintain—against all the views propagated by laissez-faire livers—that in God's sight, parents do have authority and their children are expected to respect it. The counselor may not opt for anything less in his dealings with families in trouble because of the lack of such respect. It is a part of the ten commandments that children must honor their fathers and mothers.

But, in it all, it is also important to note that the time will come when they will be set free from the restrictions now imposed on them, and, no more live like "slaves" (interestingly, an accusation made by more than one child chafing under his parents' authority!). Maturity, the counselor may indicate, comes in a proper way when one has endured the conditions of minority successfully; not when he has rebelled against them.

Verse 4 continues the figure: "when the time had fully come." What time? That set by the father (v. 2) for the son to emerge from the state of minority and come into his own. That time, for God's people, was when God sent forth Christ, incarnate, Who perfectly fulfilled the law (both in its demands and by receiving its punishments in the place of guilty sinners). He came to redeem those who were under law (v. 5) so that they might be adopted as "sons." As sons, whom God treats fully as such (though adopted), through the Spirit poured into their hearts (Cf. Romans 5:5), they learn to love God and cry out to Him as true sons do "Abba" (Father, or possibly "Daddy"). Well, if that is true of an heir, and the analogy holds, Christians, who by definition possess the Spirit, are no longer slaves to the old elementary order of things, but are now mature sons and heirs of God (v. 7).

God sent forth Christ in the fullness of time. Like the father who has set the date when he will consider his son mature, and no longer a minor, so too God sets and acts according to His schedule. Christ came not a

8 Once, however, you served as slaves of those who by nature are not gods.

---

minute too soon or too late; He was on time. That is important for the children of God to recognize. Many counselees get into trouble because they fail to schedule, or, of they do, they fail to keep to the schedule. Good counselors will be able to note that if God makes schedules, sets times, and keeps to them, surely His children need to do so as well.

More closely to the meaning of the passage: Christians are heirs. God has not only saved them, but has given them all things in Christ. Many counselees complain about their lot, much like the Psalmist in Psalm 73. But, even if the blessings that one receives in this life are principally spiritual and not material, there is an indescribable inheritance coming to every one of the children of God. That is something to help counselees look forward to. Certainly, the apostle Paul found this forward look not only comforting but enervating, even when he compared it with the severe trials that he was suffering (II Cor. 4:16,17).

It is often important to remind counselees of their legal standing before God: they are "sons." And because they are, they are legal heirs. But, as important as that may be, they are also sons who possess the Holy Spirit of love. If they haven't experienced much of the love that makes them refer to their heavenly Father in intimate terms (like "Abba"), there is something wrong in their relationship to Him. Either their faith is ingenuine or they are ungrateful for their redemption and adoption. Helping them focus on that relationship is a good beginning, as they recognize the privileges of adoption here as well as hereafter. Explaining these to them may have much to do with acquiring right attitudes toward life and toward the God Who controls it.

Argument Six: Don't turn back to the weak and the pitiful things you left. Consider now verses 8-11. In these verses Paul clearly contrasts the old ways in paganism and corrupt Judaism with what the Galatian Christians have in Christ. Do you want to return to idolatry, he asks? You were once slaves of pagan gods that were not really gods at all. They couldn't hear your prayers or answer them, because they didn't exist. There was no hope or future in living for them. They did nothing for you in this world and will be dethroned in the world to come. How can you Galatians desert the true and living God to go back to this? Now, you know God—the true One. The difference between what you had and what you have now should be clear to you.

9   But now that you know God (or rather, that you are known by God), how can you turn back to those weak and pitiful elements? Do you want to become enslaved by them once again?
10   You are keeping days and months and seasons and years—
11   I am afraid that I have labored among you in vain!

Not only did you come to know the true God, but in His mercy and grace, He was the One Who first fixed His concern on you and saved you so that you could know and serve Him (v. 9a). Well, then, have you forgotten what it was like in the past when you served gods that were not gods? Think! Remember! If you do, you will see the contrast. I ask you, How can you turn back? That is Paul's argument here.

People who become enamored with error because of its novelty, etc., need to be reminded of the place from which they came, and that the error they now are ready to embrace will do nothing more than take them back to those old ways. It is easy to forget what it used to be like. Counselors will make good use, therefore, of the important means of resisting hurtful error that Paul employs by calling counselees to remember and contrast what they now have in Christ with whatever it is they are flirting with that is not truly Christian.

Paul continues by calling the old ways "weak and pitiful," elements (basic teachings of falsehood) that enslave. The old rituals, fears, ways of paganism; the old ideas that you could be saved by keeping the traditions of the fathers and the laws of apostate Judaism, these—a host of ideas, presuppositions, views that when it comes to bringing salvation, meaning and purpose to life—prove to be utterly weak and miserably pitiful. Paul did not have any hesitancy when it came to describing false belief for what it is; nor should you. It is only when you characterize false ways as impotent, and call on counselees to recognize the difference between them and what Christ has done for them that they will awaken.

Paul knows that they have been captured again by these old ways and were once more becoming slaves of ritual and ceremony: they are keeping (observing) days and months and seasons and years. The Jewish calendar had been imposed on them. They were now becoming subject to its ordinances, celebrations and ceremonies. These things were all types and shadows of Christ and His spiritual kingdom; to return to them was a throwback. It would not do. Paul wonders, "Did I labor among you for nothing?" He fears that might be the case. However, as we have already observed, since this letter was preserved and sent out to all the churches, it

12I beg you brothers, become what I am; after all I became like you. You didn't wrong me in any way.

13 You know that it was because of physical sickness that I announced the good news to you in the first place.

---

is clear that the churches—or at least some of them—must have responded positively.

Paul does not hesitate to argue from his own efforts. Nor is it wrong for you to say from time to time to a counselee who is not working properly at his part of the counseling process, "I'm afraid that I've put in all this time and energy for nothing." After all, the time of God's servants is valuable. While one counselee dawdles about making requisite changes, to the frustration of all involved, another could be using his time and place in making real progress. "Why does the fig tree cumber the ground when it bears no fruit?" There comes a time to cut it down. But Paul has not yet given up on the Galatians. Like the gardener in Christ's parable, he will "dig it and dung it" once more (by the way, that is a pretty good description of pastoral ministry!). Nor should you easily give up on your counselees.

Argument Seven: Don't undo what you did in the past. While you are remembering, thinking of the difference that Christ made, remember too those days when you first heard me preach the gospel. That is Paul's next plea. Become free from all that Judaistic legalism, as I did. After all, I became like you (I live like a gentile and not like a Jew). How strange it is that I a Jew have become like a gentile while you, who are in the main gentiles, want to become like Jews! It is strange, but it is common, to find people—even Christian people—going after something that intrigues them because they have never been a part of it or experienced it. Here is a counselor who has come out of a background of psychotherapeutic training and practice of one sort or another, who now sees it as weak and pitiful in its ability to help, and has turned to biblical counseling alone. On the other hand, here is his counselee who has never been involved in the slavery of psychological counseling toying with it even though he comes out of a thoroughly taught biblical background. People are simply perverse! But often they don't realize it until you point it out to them as Paul did (v. 12).

The reason, remember, that I stopped there in your midst and preached the gospel in the first place was because I had become ill (v. 13). Indeed, you might have despised me because my illness became a burden

41

14   And even though my physical condition was a trial to you, you neither despised nor disdained me, but rather received me as an angel from God, as Christ Jesus Himself!

15   What happened, then, to your gladness? I testify that, if it had been possible, you would have gouged your eyes and given them to me.

16   So now, have I become your enemy by being truthful with you?

17   The zeal that they show toward you isn't good; instead they want to alienate you so that you will become zealous for them.

---

to you. But, quite to the contrary, you treated me like an angel from God; no, let me say more—like Jesus Christ Himself. You didn't wrong me. You were kind and gracious to me. You were so glad to see me: what has happened to that gladness? Why has it disappeared so quickly? Why, at that time, if it had been possible, you were so grateful to me for bringing the gospel to you that you would have gouged out your eyes and given them to me to cure my eye trouble (vv. 14,15). How is it then that I have become an enemy? Was it because I spoke the truth?

This personal appeal is moving. Not only does it tell us much about the apostle's illness, his thorn in the flesh, but it tells us that his eye condition must have been so serious at the time he was passing through Galatia that he could not go on. It tells us that he not only stopped, but he had to obtain medical treatment which, at some cost of time (and perhaps money), the Galatians gladly gave him. The warm relationship with Paul, that was the milieu in which the Galatian churches were born, was a strong argument. *Remember*, says Paul. Don't let these smooth-talking Judaizers break up this fine relationship we once had around the truth.

Indeed, says Paul, let's examine the zeal that these troublemakers seem to have for you. Is it good? Does it spring from noble motives? Absolutely not!. They are trying to alienate you and me so that you will focus your whole attention on them. They want you for their own (v. 17). They have an agenda. I want you to be zealous, but for good reasons—not for the wrong ones. And, I don't want you to make up to me only when I am present; that is hypocrisy. No, if you are zealous for me and the gospel, it must be zeal that lasts and continues even when I have departed.

Counseling changes likewise must remain after formal counseling is over. It is of little value for counselees to do right only so long as the counselor is watching over them. After it has been completed, they must be able to sustain new ways and gains made while counseling. That will happen only if the counselor is careful not to make the counselee dependent on him. How may he avoid this? Well, in a number of ways. First, he

18 It is always a fine thing to be zealous for a good reason, and not only when I am present with you.
19 My children, over whom I travail again until Christ is formed in you,
20 I wish I could be present with you right now, to change my tone, because I am perplexed about you!
   21 Tell me, you who want to be under the law, don't you listen to the law?
22 It is written that Abraham had two sons, one by the slave and the other by the free woman.
23 But the son of the slave was born according to the flesh, and the son born of the free woman through the promise.

---

must give weekly homework assignments to the counselee to follow when among his family members, at work and elsewhere, so that he makes the changes on his own (with the Spirit's aid, of course; but not the counselor's). Secondly, the counselor, before dismissing the counselee, will in many cases ask the counselee to write out his own homework assignments (and do them). Thirdly, often, the counselor will set up a six week checkup after counseling sessions have been completed to make sure that the principles and practices adopted in making changes that please God are still intact. If they are not, he will investigate why they are not and rectify the situation.

But back to the text. Paul feels like a pregnant mother about to give birth to the Galatian churches. Turning the figure around quite rapidly, he says that he wants Christ formed in *them*. It is almost as if he must start all over again. I realize that my tone is somewhat harsh, and I wish I could be there among you seeing a change in your thinking as the result of what I am saying so that I could soften that tone, he says. Paul didn't know quite how to address them; he didn't know how they would respond. He was perplexed.

The warmth of this section tells us much of the love of Paul (in Christ) for his converts. How wonderful it would be if the love of each counselor for those to whom he ministers were equally displayed. A true pastor's heart is necessary for working with God's children. Paul had it. The shepherdly note rings out loudly in these verses. If you do not have it, counselor, you will not spend the time to reclaim those who are about to defect. In counseling, you will meet many in that very same state. You must be able to strike the right note of a serious, clear, at times even harsh tone, combined with the wooing note. Learn from the great apostle.

Argument Eight: The Allegory. The rabbis were fond of allegory. In

43

24 Now these things may be allegorized: these are two covenants, one indeed coming from Mount Sinai (which is Hagar) bearing children who will be slaves.

25 Now Hagar is Mount Sinai which is in Arabia; she corresponds to the present Jerusalem; she is in slavery with her children.

26 But the Jerusalem above is free, who is our mother.

27 It is written:

> **Be glad, barren woman who does not give birth,**
> **Break out and shout, you who are not in labor;**
> **The desolate woman has more children**
> **Than the woman who has a husband!**

---

general, it was not a Christian preacher's way of speaking. But here Paul turns the Judaizer's guns on themselves. They use allegory, do they? Well, let me draw out an allegory for you that makes clear what is happening to you Galatians.

You want to put yourself under the law as a way of salvation, do you? OK, listen to what you find in the law. Abraham's two sons were born of two women, one free, one a slave. One was born of flesh—that is in the ordinary way. The other of promise in an extraordinary way. Let me allegorize these facts for you (v. 24). There are two covenants, one coming from Mt. Sinai (that Hagar stands for), and her children are slaves—just as all those who put themselves under the law for salvation become slaves to it. Hagar represents Mt. Sinai in Arabia, and she also corresponds to the present, physical Jerusalem here on earth. Both she and her children are in slavery.

Then, in contrast, there is a Jerusalem that is heavenly, free—*our* mother. Sarah's desolation has, according to God's promise, which has now been fulfilled, resulted in more children than the other's. You are like Isaac, children of promise, not children of the flesh who are slaves. In Christ, you are free. But just as the fleshly son persecuted the one born of the Spirit, so too is it now. These men are persecuting both you and me by their slanderous words and their destructive acts. The Scripture says "Throw them out!" I expect you to do so. They cannot serve or inherit the promise together; they are as antithetical to one another as those in this allegory. We belong to the free woman; not to the slave. Get your thinking straight.

A counselor may often turn the very kinds of arguments that others use around and use them on them instead. Just keep that in mind when necessary to do something to dislodge errors that a counselee has bought

28 Now you, brothers, like Isaac, are children of promise.

29 But just as then the one born according to the flesh persecuted the one who was born according to the Spirit, so too it is now.

30 But what does the Scripture say?

> **Throw out the slave and her son;**
> **by no means shall the son of the slave share the inheritance of**
> **the son of the free woman.**

31 So, brothers, we aren't children of the slave but of the free woman.

---

from someone else. Ask, "What did he say?" When you have a pretty good idea of how he presented his error, if possible, say, "Well, two can play at that game. Suppose we take that kind of argument and use it to evaluate what you were taught..." That is often a powerful response to persons who have been confused by those that teach error.

CHAPTER 5

1 It was for freedom that Christ freed us; stand firm therefore, and don't subject yourselves again to a yoke of slavery.

2 Mark these words: I, Paul, tell you that if you are circumcised Christ will be of no profit to you.

Though the fifth chapter of Galatians is the chapter in which the third, practical section begins, there is a conclusion to part two at the outset (vv. 1-6). It was for freedom—the very thing that the false teachers wanted to rob the Galatians of—that Christ freed them from the law as a means of salvation. Freedom in Christ means also to be freed from the law's curse. In Christ, they are no longer children of the bondwoman. Therefore, he pleads, "don't subject yourselves again to a yoke of slavery."

How heart-wrenching it is to see someone heading back into the very life-style from which you have worked to extricate him! Paul felt it keenly; everything about this letter indicates that fact. And, the same error is seen in counseling all the time. You too will feel disappointment. People willfully determine to return to those ineffectual ways of living from which Christ has freed them. A principal task of counselors, therefore, is not merely to point out what is happening whenever they encounter such retrogression in a counselee, but, like Paul, to plead with him not to continue in it. Paul urges, "stand firm." But that is precisely the problem with many; the moment pressure is applied back at home, at work, or elsewhere in an environment in which your influence is minimal and the influence of others is stronger, the counselee buckles under the pressure. How can you help him stand firm?

Well, you can give him (in detail, as Paul did) answers to all the questions posed by those who object to the course that you are prescribing. Moreover (again, like Paul), you can fortify him with positive arguments for following the proper biblical course. And once more, (as Paul did), you can warn him about the consequences of not listening to Scripture. Indeed, that is exactly how Paul concludes: by warning the reader.

"Mark these words," says Paul. He is about to warn in the most emphatic terms. 'I, Paul, tell you... "What does this kind of language signify? Paul is asserting every bit of his personal and apostolic authority. "I Paul"—for all that you have known me to be to you, and for all that I have reiterated about my divine commission—tell you what I am about to say.

3   I testify again to every person who is circumcised that he is obligated to keep the entire law.

If you ever listened to me, if you have the slightest inclination to do so again, *then hear what I am about to say.*

The summary statement by which he capsulizes all he has been saying follows: "if you are circumcised Christ will be of no profit to you." That is a powerful statement. It is set forth in the form of an antithesis: either it is circumcision (that is, all that it currently stood for in Judaism as a way of salvation) or Christ (and all He stands for). You can't have it both ways. Frequently, as a counselor, you must require your counselee to **choose**. The options in biblical counseling are, as in Paul's biblical writings, always two: Christ—or something else. Many counselees will want it both ways; Christ, however, insists on a choice.

If one puts himself under the law as a means of salvation (the false Jewish notion of the day), he is turning to another gospel, which is not another of the same kind, but is, in fact, only *bad* news. Christ came to fulfill the law; something they could not do. But, His work is of no profit to those who trust in their own merit. I pointed out to you, Paul reminds them, that when you take the apostate Jewish route of circumcision, you are obligated to keep the entire law. If you offend in one point, you are cursed. But who, in his right mind, will stand up and say he has never violated a commandment of God? The very idea is absurd. When you can lead a counselee to see, not only the danger of proceeding on an unbiblical course of action, but also the manifest absurdity of doing so, you have added a powerful incentive to your plea. Few counselees want to look stupid.

It is impossible to serve two masters—the one saying, "keep the commandments" and the other saying, "You can't, but, there is hope: I kept them for My own." Paul warns that those who wish to be justified by keeping the law have broken their relationship to Christ; they "have fallen away from grace." By moving from a position that says salvation is by grace, through faith, they now say one can be justified by works. They have turned their back on the Savior; they have opted, instead, for self-salvation. Were they saved and then lost? No. Paul's warns that any who genuinely reject Christ and justification by faith, though having outwardly professed it, never were saved in the first place. For those, who are genuine Christians, but confused, perhaps following others, his plea is "turn back from your wandering ways."

4   You who want to be justified by law have broken your relationship with Christ; you have fallen away from grace.
5   Yet we, in the Spirit by faith, eagerly await the righteousness for which we hope.

There will always be two kinds of counselees, just as there are always two kinds of church members: those who are genuine and those who are not. The genuine possess the Spirit; the others do not. There is hope for change among the first; none among the latter, until they are converted. Counseling involves obedience to divine commandments. Those who refuse even to attempt such obedience frequently turn out to be false professors; those who try, though they often fail, usually are genuine. It will turn out that a given number of counselees, though professing faith in Christ, will, during the process, give you good reason to become suspicious of their salvation. While no counselor may judge hearts, from the fruit (or lack of it) in the counselee's life, nevertheless, you must make a *functional* judgment about him. From a functional judgment (as opposed to a judgment about his actual heart condition), the counselor may say, "I see no evidence of saving graces at work in his heart, and, following unsuccessful church discipline, should it be such, I must treat him as unsaved." Counseling gets down to cases. It deals with people in terms of their values, actions, beliefs and attitudes. It is personal. It is not abstract. Paul always dealt with his counselees in an interpersonal manner; he did not hesitate to express his own concerns and reactions to them. Such counseling, therefore, comes closer to uncovering those who are genuine and those who are not than any other ministerial activity, thus separating the good fish from the bad. For this reason, counseling will, in many cases, issue in the process of church discipline.

In contrast to those who have fallen from the teaching of grace (v. 4), Paul says we who trust in Jesus Christ and possess His Spirit eagerly "await the righteousness for which we hope." That means, they are awaiting here in this life greater conformity to the will of God, but, especially, the day in which all sin will be removed from them and they will not only be *declared* perfectly righteous in Christ, but will be *made* as righteous as He. When the Bible uses the word "hope," it refers not to the hope-so hope of our day. It means a confident expectation of something that inevitably will take place because God has promised it. The only thing that makes it "hope" is that the event promised yet remains future. But, the hope is *firm*.

6   In Christ Jesus neither circumcision nor uncircumcision is of any account, but only faith working through love.

7   You were running well; who cut in on you so that you no longer obey the truth?

Then, capping it all off, Paul writes that, in the final analysis, it isn't whether you are circumcised or not that makes the difference (he himself had been), but whether you have faith that works through love. Here, the three graces, faith, love and works, that appear frequently in Paul, once again appear. They cannot be separated. True faith (the root) always leads to works (the shoot), followed, in time, by love (the fruit). Whenever these are present, even if in a minimal way, it is clear that the Spirit has been at work in a counselee's life. This conclusion is also transitional and leads naturally to the final section of the epistle, the practical one in which the loving works of faith are discussed.

Paul asks a question, framed in language from the Olympic games (thinking here of the foot races): "**You were running well; who cut in on you?** (v. 7)" That they had quickly turned from freedom in Christ to a doctrine of works righteousness occasioned amazement in Paul, as we have seen. He is still struck by the fact; the question shows something of his amazement at that desertion. The question seems rhetorical (Paul knew it was the Judaizing false brothers who had brought about this condition, though he didn't know exactly which ones), designed, as most rhetorical questions, not for purposes of information gathering, but to make the reader think about himself. You were, Paul says, running the race well until someone, against all the rules of the track, cut in on you so as to hinder you and, possibly, trip you up. The wording is felicitous and still may be used profitably in counseling whenever you recognize the evil influence of others leading your counselee astray. "Things were going well. You got off to a great start in counseling and were, thereafter, running well. But someone has cut in on you!"

The effect of this influence is expressed in the latter half of verse 7: the Galatians were no longer obeying the truth. They were listening to and following error. This error could mean confusion for them (presuming their previous good start on the race shows the genuineness of their conversion) and damnation for their children and others to whom their churches ministered who would be taught to trust in ceremonies and good works for their salvation. Obedience to the truth—or its opposite—has powerful practical implications. Never allow anyone to tell you that what

8   This persuasion didn't come from the One Who called you.
9   A little leaven leavens the whole lump.

---

one believes and how he practices those beliefs is a matter of indifference, or, perhaps, a matter that effects himself alone. Counselees must be shown the consequences of stumbling when they ought to be racing well.

Paul plainly indicates the antithesis between truth, as taught by him, and error as taught by the Judaizers when he declares: **"This persuasion didn't come from the One Who called you."** There was an alien source. And it couldn't be allowed to have its way unchallenged. As Paul says, **A little leaven leavens the whole lump.** Someone said to me recently, concerning false teaching "Oh well, it's only a peripheral issue." Well, in some ways it was, I could agree. But even that peripheral issue, worked out in certain contexts, as I demonstrated, could have a disastrous outcome. All error, in one way or another, is pernicious; none could be more so than this Judaizing substitute for the gospel.

Paul now speaks more moderately about the Galatians, expressing confidence, at least in the leadership of the church, that they will agree with what he has been writing and will judge the one—whoever he was—in error and, thus, he would be heard no longer. His strong words have to do with those who are perverting the gospel. Indeed, in verse 12, he says if they are so handy with the knife, "I wish they would castrate themselves!" Paul is probably speaking figuratively, meaning, "I wish they would eliminate their capacity to do any more harm." But, the figure, nonetheless, is a powerful one. Counselors may not be anxious to do so, but there are times to express just such attitudes toward those who are spreading infectious error that is destroying their counselee and the lives of others. Paul points out that if he were still preaching circumcision (salvation by law-keeping) as he once did, he would not be persecuted; in that case, there would be no stumbling block in his message—the cross would not be central. But, he is persecuted and there are those who stumble precisely because he no longer preaches salvation by works and ceremonies. Instead, he preaches the gospel: salvation through the cross.

Now, for the results of freedom or bondage in the life; that is what he is about to consider. If you want to know the truth or error of what is preached, then take a hard look at what each of the two views produces.

What God called you to, he says, is freedom; freedom from the obligations of law-keeping for salvation, freedom from the curse of the law in consequence of breaking at law. It is freedom from the power of sin in the

10 I am confident about you in the Lord that you won't think differently; but rather that the one who is troubling you will bear his judgment, whoever he may be.

11 But if I, brothers, still preach circumcisions, then why am I still being persecuted? If that were the case then the stumbling block of the cross would be removed.

12 I wish that those who are unsettling you would castrate themselves!

13 You were called to freedom, brothers; only don't allow the flesh to take advantage of this freedom. Instead, through love serve one another like slaves.

14 The entire law is summed up in this one statement: **Love your neighbor as yourself**.

---

life and freedom to keep the law out of love and gratitude for salvation rather than to be saved. Since you are free to do righteousness, free from slavery to sin, you must not allow the flesh to take advantage of you (v. 13). What is this "flesh?" As I have shown in depth in the book, *The War Within*, which contains a rather detailed study of this subject as it is worked out by Paul in chapters 6 and 7 of Romans, "flesh" means the body as it has been habituated by the sinful nature with which we were born. It is the yielding of the members of the body to sin, by which habits are developed that are out of accord with God's will. It is "sin in the members." When one comes into the new life of Christ, he must contend with many habit patterns, replacing them throughout his lifetime with righteous, biblical alternatives. Here, Paul warns against the habitual patterns that continually seek expression in a Christian's life. To let them take advantage of you is neither right nor inevitable. The particular kind of fleshly activity about which he seems to be thinking is self-concern, rather than concern for others. This would follow naturally from the doctrine of self-salvation with which the Galatians were toying. People who look to themselves for salvation, spend inordinate amounts of time introspectively cultivating their lives as self-salvationists do, are most likely to fall into it. They rarely look toward others. Instead, Paul says, "Let your freedom in Christ not mean license, but see to it that it issues in serving one another." After all, brotherly love, as we read throughout the New Testament (but especially in I John) is strong evidence of salvation.

The entire law is summed up in the statement "Love your neighbor as yourself." You want to keep the law, says Paul. O.K. Let your freedom in Christ result in the freedom from self and freedom to show love to others. Jesus summed up the law as loving God and loving neighbor. How is

15 But if you bite and devour one another, look out or you will be consumed by one another.

---

it that Paul can reduce it to only one of those propositions? Probably because if you consider God your most important Neighbor—One with Whom you have to do—you can see love for *others*, including God, as the sum of the law. Here, however, his concern focuses principally on dissension in the Galatian church (v. 15). "Stop eating each other up" is the message.

How appropriate a word to so many counselees! That is a vividly accurate description of what is going on in so many homes and churches—people are biting and devouring one another. Husbands and wives are particularly apt at doing so. Here, it is dissension created by false doctrine, it would seem, that is Paul's principal interest. But it is interesting to note that one of the consequences of error is destructive attitudes and actions toward others. This is inevitable. And it can consume a church or home so as to destroy it. That is always true of the introduction of a false way of salvation into the midst of a group of Christians, whether that group is a home, a Christian school or a Church. The flesh is always nurtured by error. It not only continues its place of control over the believer, but in the form of error, leads to new and different sinful habits. The flesh, therefore, must be defeated. But it is precisely those old habits (the old "you") that, in one way or another, were in line with the doctrine of self-salvation. That is why this error, introduced into the Galatian church, was so pernicious: it drove Christians who played around with it back into the old ways that they had been endeavoring to put off. As Paul says in I Corinthians 15:33, "Evil companions corrupt [even] *good* habits." That is to say, even after one has put off an old pattern of life, he may revert to it under an evil influence.

That was happening here. And, it will happen to your counselees. This entire book of Galatians is a strong entreaty to the counselor to consider not only the counselee who sits before you, but whoever else has the most profound influence upon him. It is an issue you may always want to explore, but especially whenever you discover retrogression to pre-christian attitudes, beliefs and behavior. Take any such material as evidence that there are outside influences for evil at work in his life.

How does one overcome the "flesh?" Paul details the matter in Romans 6-8, of course, but here gives a three verse summary of all he says there (vv. 16-18). Here is the open secret of sanctification: "walk by

16 Now I tell you, walk by the Spirit and it is certain that you won't accomplish the desires of the flesh.

17 The flesh's desires are contrary to those of the Spirit, and the Spirit's are contrary to those of the flesh. They are in opposition to one another so that you won't do what you want to do.

18 But if you are led by the Spirit, you aren't under law.

---

the Spirit and it is certain that you will not obey the desires of the flesh." The two, he continues, are "in opposition" to one another. What the flesh desires is the opposite of what the Spirit desires. So, one finds himself not doing the things that he wants to do to serve the Spirit. The Christian is engaged in war within. Have you ever heard a counselee say something like this, "Before I was a Christian, in some ways, things seemed easier. Now, I have a new problem: I find myself at war with myself." Of course, and good! That is evidence of the Spirit at work within, challenging the corrupt patterns of life habituated into your body by the sinful nature with which you were born.

It was easier before conversion because there was no opposition. Now there is a constant demand by the Spirit to change. Your old person is now frustrated; he doesn't get his way as he used to. And he kicks! But, if the Spirit leads you into biblical living, there should be no question about whether you are still under the law for salvation; you are already saved or the Spirit would not be leading you in those ways.

Now, says Paul, let's consider some of the works of the flesh (N.B., he calls them "works" because, in one's attempt to save himself through good works, this is what he produces). They are apparent, he observes. That is, they are always found with the self-salvation group, sooner or later emerging as evidence of the futile way of self-salvation through ceremonies and works. The person doing such things may not be aware of the fact; after all, the heart is "deceitful." He may envision himself a paragon of righteousness. But, to others, his attitudes and his ways are apparent. The list that follows is not exhaustive, nor is it necessary for us to pause and look at each word. The exegetical commentaries do a fine job of this. A couple observations, however, profitably may be made. Counselees who doubt the sinfulness of certain ways that they are living may be brought to this passage in order to examine those ways. Laying their practices alongside the list is often useful in bringing conviction of sin. Moreover, that jealousy, strife, rages, selfishness (especially today!), rivalries, divisions and envy find their place together with idolatry, sor-

19 Now it is apparent that the works of the flesh are sexual immorality, uncleanness, sensuality,
20 idolatry, sorcery, enmities, strife, jealousy, rages, selfishness, rivalries, divisions, sectarianism,
21 envy, drunkenness, carousing and things like these; I warn you (just as I previously did) that those who practice such things will not inherit God's empire.

---

cery, adultery drunkenness, "and things like these," should give some, who think lightly of those problems, a moment's pause. God considers all these (not just the grosser ones) "works of the flesh!"

If a person's life is characterized by these things, says Paul,; if he "practices" them, he warns, that person is lost. He will not inherit God's kingdom. He is not a true child of Abraham, a son, heir to all the promises.

Now, it is important to distinguish between occasional indulgences in acts of the flesh and a life-style characterized by the same. The word "practice," toward the end of verse 21 (rather than "do") more accurately expresses the Greek original. The force of this word is that this is the ordinary life-style that one practices or of which he approves. Not that he indulges in all of these vices (he may never get drunk, but may have envy that causes untold heartache for others), but that he *practices* those in which he does. There is a warning here that it is only fair to issue to those who, in your judgment, seem to be *practicing* some of the works of the flesh—"you are probably not saved." If that seems to be the case, you must cease counseling and work toward the conversion of your (now former) counselee.

Now, in contrast, Paul sets forth (again, non-exhaustively) the "fruit of the Spirit." By "fruit" he means the result of the work of the Holy Spirit within. While we may take credit for the works of the flesh, we may not take credit for the fruit of the Spirit for which He must be praised. That doesn't mean that there is no work on your counselee's part in cultivating and harvesting this fruit. Indeed, elsewhere, Paul speaks of the "pursuit" of such fruit (I Timothy 6:11). It is a joint venture in which the Spirit provides both the desire and the ability for you to do as He pleases (Cf. Philippians 2:13). Neither extreme of the swing of the pendulum is biblical. The Christian does not produce righteousness by his own, unaided efforts. Nor does the Spirit produce it *for* him, *instead of* him, Together, as the Spirit gives wisdom, encouragement and power, the fruit grows. Christian responsibility thus is not impaired.

22 But the Spirit's fruit is love, joy, peace, patience, kindness, goodness, faithfulness
23 meekness, self-control. There is no law against such things.
24 Now those who belong to Christ Jesus have crucified the flesh with its passions and desires.

Again, it is necessary only to comment on the fruit. If you want more on it, see my book, *A Theology of Counseling*. Once more, the Christian may examine his life as to whether such fruit is present. If it is not, even in small measure, then he is not a believer. If it is, even in small measure, he is truly a child of God (disobedient, uninstructed, confused—or whatever—nevertheless, a believer). There is no law against such things, says Paul. Of course not! The law forbids the works of the flesh but encourages the fruit of the Spirit. It is not, then, that the law is bad; on the contrary. The law encourages the very same things that the Spirit produces in the Christian. They are not opposed; they are truly in sync. It is the very works that the Judaizers are doing while attempting to obey the law), the works of the flesh, that the law opposed.

See how expertly Paul has turned the issue around so that the very weapons employed by the enemy are those that blast him out of his bunker? The same sort of ability to reason from Scripture must be developed by the Christian counselor. Unhappily, from time to time, he will find himself in debate with his counselees. Of course, Rogerians, and counselors of other sorts, will find such methodology not only unsettling but shocking. Nevertheless, at times it is absolutely essential to do precisely what Paul does. Notice, however, he does not so much tell the counselee that he is wrong as he chiefly places the onus on those who "cut in" and are "leavening" the church. That is the place to carry on the debate with your counselee, as often as possible: with the arguments of those who teach error. Sometimes, it may even be necessary to actually debate them in the presence of the counselee, so that the truth may emerge for him. At any rate, Paul is debating the Judaizers when he declares, "There is no law against such things."

Those who belong to Christ have crucified the flesh. The flesh was dealt a powerful blow by the cross of Christ when the Spirit regenerated the believer. It was crucified with Him. It no longer need reign in the believer's life. It's passions and desires ought, as a result, to be minimized more and more as the fruit of the Spirit appears. Here, again, Paul is giving them evidence that progress in the life of true believers is brought

> **25** If we live by the Spirit, let us also walk by the Spirit.
> 26 Let us not become conceited, challenging one another, envying one another.

---

about by the presence and work of the Spirit Who dwells within. They began with the Spirit; they must continue with Him, not with themselves, in the driver's seat. So, if life came by the Spirit, continue to "walk" by His wisdom and power. The walk of the Christian is his life-style. The Christian life is Spirit-driven rather than flesh-driven (v. 25).

All of this applies to them as they were now carrying on. Once more Paul stresses the need to avoid the divisive works of the flesh mentioned in verse 26. These things, the result of those who were "troubling" them, must cease. And, they would, were the Galatians to return to the simple gospel which, alone, leads to the work of grace.

CHAPTER 6

1 Brothers, even if a person is caught in some trespass, you who have the Spirit should restore him in a spirit of meekness, watching out for yourself so that you won't be tempted too.

I have published a book, *Ready to Restore*, devoted to the counseling implications found in the first verse of this chapter. Obviously, therefore, I can do little more than enumerate some of the conclusions that I reached there.

The first verse, and the four that follow, directly address the counseling situation. If a brother becomes so entangled in a trespass that he is unable to extricate himself, and unable to manifest the Spirit's fruit, the Christian who recognizes his condition (it doesn't say only the pastor or elders of the church) is obligated to restore him. That means that it is not optional to do so. It also means that one does not wait until asked for help; he offers it. He takes the initiative and becomes involved. That may not always be to the liking of the sinning Christian, but it is definitely an obligation that must be fulfilled whether appreciated or not.

The one who is "caught" needs to be freed from his sinful ways so that he may be **restored**. That is a key term. It is used of fishermen mending their nets and of physicians mending broken bones. The idea is to restore the useless, injured limb or torn net to usefulness again. Christians seem always to be complaining that only a few do all the work. Well, it may be that if they were to expend the energy they use complaining on attempting to restore those toward whom those complaints are aimed, they might find relief.

Notice, also, to whom this directive is addressed: **you who have the Spirit**. The Christian is not to send erring brothers or sisters to unbelieving counselors. Those who possess the Holy Spirit, are qualified to help another. True, they may not know much about how to do so, but they have the basic equipment. And, through availing themselves of such volumes as this, they will discover ways of improving. The task of counseling, formally, belongs to the elders of the church; informally, to every Christian (See *Competent to Counsel* for details). It has not been said often or loudly enough that the believer is not to seek the "counsel of the ungodly" (Psalm One). In Galatians 6:1 Paul positively, asserts the same—it is a *Christian* who is to dislodge those who are trapped under a load of sin.

2   Bear one another's burdens and so fulfill Christ's law.

That is what it means to "bear his burden" (v. 2) until he is restored to a position of usefulness in the Church and able to carry his share of the "load "(v. 5). One temporarily lifts the burden, so that the trapped Christian may wriggle out from beneath the boulder under which he is trapped, not in order to assume his share of the load in addition to his own, but to free the brother once again to assume a responsible place in the body of Christ.

"But," says an immature brother or sister, "I wouldn't know where to begin." Well, Paul doesn't say you can't get help. In many situations that would be the wise thing to do. But don't throw your responsibility to restore off on someone else. If, in God's providence, you were the one to discover your fellow Christian's problem, and you initiated the restoration process, keep working at it. Bring in others *only to assist*, as you continue. Otherwise, you are likely never to learn.

Two factors will make your effort easier. First, you must approach the sinning Christian in a spirit of "meekness." Meekness is difficult to define; it is more easily understood by describing its opposite. To say to a brother caught in sin, "Well, I guess this was to be expected. After all, how many times have I said...," is to kick him when he is down. No, any such superior attitude is the opposite of meekness. Meekness acts more like this: "Brother, I am here not because I consider myself better than you, but because in Galatians 6, God tells me to come. As a matter of fact, I may need you to help me out of some difficulty in the future."

The other consideration that will make the counseling obligation easier is to heed the warning not to fall into the same temptation that the one whom you are attempting to extricate did. Some, all too readily become enmeshed in sexual sin when trying to help another out of it. That is why a third party should always be present when the problem is even remotely connected with sexual matters. The Name of Christ is muddied whenever such a fall occurs. Even as I write, after weeks of tedious and disheartening effort, I am only now beginning to clear up a case of such sin by a counselor, the effects of which are widespread.

Counselor, consider this too: if every Christian is required to counsel entangled believers whom God providentially brings into their purview, then during counseling, you will often uncover situations in which your counselee has a responsibility to counsel someone. In such cases, having

3 If somebody thinks that he is something when he is nothing, he deceives himself.

4 But let each one test his own work; then he will have something to boast about in himself alone, rather than comparing himself with another.

---

helped restore him, you may find yourself, through him, counseling another. In those instances, your counseling of the first person having been completed, you will find it necessary to teach him what to do to help his brother or sister.

To bear another's burden (in order to help restore him) is to fulfill Christ's law. That is, of course, the law of love. Love is the sum of the commandments and of the fruit of the Spirit. Such love, we have seen, is not generated by us but is poured into our hearts by the Holy Spirit (Romans 5:5) at the time of regeneration. To walk on the other side when a Christian is in trouble is to fail to love one's neighbor who, in addition, is a brother in Christ. You are worse than those who preceded the coming of the good Samaritan. It is not possible, therefore, for a Christian to "beg off" from this responsibility.

In keeping with the quality of meekness that should accompany all counseling, the counselor must not think he is something when, in reality, he is "nothing" (v. 3). So much for self-esteem teaching! Everything you have to offer by way of help is from God's Word; you didn't dream it up. Where, then, is your right to boast? (Cf. v. 14). It is a curse to the successful counselor who allows success to go to his head. God will have none of that. The counselor is nothing; as John the Baptist said, Christ "must increase" as the counselor decreases. It is the task of the counselor to point the counselee to Christ and away from Himself. The counselor who fails to do this, attempts to rob God of some of His glory in order to allocate it to himself. He also tends to make counselees dependent on himself rather than on God.

The counselor who becomes puffed up because he thinks, "Thank God I am not like the counselee I am counseling," thinks wrongly (v. 4; cf. also the story of the Pharisee and the tax collector in Luke 18). He ought not compare himself with him, nor even with another counselor who may not be so successful as he. His business, says Paul, is to continually test what he himself is doing, as he analyzes it over and over, in order to become more Christian and proficiently biblical in his living and counseling. If what he is doing stands the acid test of Scripture, then he will have something to be thankful for, and he may rightly boast about how God has

5   Each person must carry his own load.

6 Now let him who is instructed in the Word share everything good that he has with the one who instructs him.

7 Don't be deceived, God isn't snubbed; whatever a person sows, that is exactly what he will reap.

---

used him.

The counselee, and the counselor alike, must each bear his own load. Neither may shift God-given responsibilities to another. The counselee is to be restored to his place in the church, pulling his own weight (incidentally, when a counselee is restored to his work in the church, that is a concrete sign that he is ready to end counseling).

This section is of the greatest importance to the counselor. It would serve him well to read and reread it often, reflecting on the many implications for counseling that may be found in it.

Moving on to verse 6, it is hard to see the immediate connection with what precedes. Perhaps there is none. Yet, if one thinks of the need to help others in trouble, it may occur to him to think of others who also may be in trouble—not in this instance of their own doing, but because of the stinginess of the Church. Verses 6 and 7 pertain to the pastor. They reveal how much a congregation should pay its pastor. He should share in **all the good things** that his congregation enjoys. That is to say, he should live on a salary commensurate with that enjoyed by those he serves. The instructor should "share" (the idea is equally) in the living style of those whom he instructs. Indeed, at times, he should do even better (Cf. I Timothy 5:17,18).

If a congregation sows inadequately, they will reap an inadequate harvest. The phrase "God is not mocked" is an interesting one. It means you can't "turn up your nose (or wipe your nose) at God and get away with it." Not to support His servants is an act of contempt toward God Himself. Here is strong encouragement for adequate support of the pastor—and more!

When counselors discuss finances with their counselees, they may use this passage, and corresponding passages in Proverbs, very profitably. In helping them set up their budgets, for instance, (a regular problem for counselors), they should stress putting the money allocated to the Lord's work at the head of everything else. In that way, by providing sufficient funds to support the pastor in a way that is in harmony with the Scriptures, they make this rule a reality. And, there are times when the counselor

8   The one who sows for his flesh will from the flesh reap corruption, but
the one who sows for the Spirit will reap eternal life.
9   Don't quit doing what is fine; at the right time we shall reap if we
don't relax our efforts.

---

must advise counselees to work toward proper support of their own pastors when others in the congregation fail to do so. At minimum, their
example may contribute to the welfare of their congregation. And, regardless of what others do or don't do, they will receive the blessings God
promises to all faithful givers. The discussion of finances, then, is a vital
part of counseling. And, it may take the form of giving properly so that
the pastor of the church to which the counselee belongs is supported adequately so that he may be able to spend the time to learn how to counsel
and, then, to engage in it.

Moving out on the example of sowing and reaping, Paul now broad-
ens the concept to all of life's activities: sow to the flesh (i.e., do those
things listed as the work of the flesh in chapter 5) and you will reap "corruption." The word corruption goes back to the fall; there would be no
such thing had Adam not sinned. Corruption of the body, the life-style,
the world around is destruction that ultimately ends in eternal damnation.
Conversely, Paul observes, sow to the Spirit (let the Spirit have His ways)
and you will reap eternal life (including all the present blessings that go
with it).

Now, says Paul, let me deal with several matters before closing this
letter. With all the controversy that is going on it is easy to give up. But,
you must not get tired of doing good. Don't slacken your efforts because
of these problems; if you continue, faithfully serving God, in time you
will reap (Paul rings the changes on the sowing and reaping metaphor). It
is so easy for counselees to give up, and thereby slacken their efforts when
others do not respond favorably to his best efforts. But he must be told
that it is Christ He serves; he is to please Him. There is not always going
to be a good outcome as far as others are concerned. But that, as disap-
pointing as it can be, is not really germane. God, whose promises don't
fail, will bring the harvest **at the right time**.

When is the "right time?" Whenever *God* sees fit to bring in the harvest; harvest time is His time. Tell your counselees that God's timetable is
not necessarily the same as theirs. Therefore, patience is required. One of
the more difficult problems that counselees have is waiting for the harvest. Yet, God has promised. This verse (v. 9b) is crucial. Use it frequently

10 So then, as the occasion arises, let us do good things for all men, but especially for the members of the household of faith.

11 Notice the large letters in which I am writing to you with my own hand.

12 Those who want to look well in the flesh are the ones who would compel you to be circumcised (for one reason only—that they may escape persecution for Christ's cross).

---

with counselees who may tend to weary of doing good when they do not reap immediate results.

Next, Paul again widens his concerns. As the occasion to do so arises, he says, let us do good things for all people; especially, however, for those of the household of faith (believers). If you tried to solve the problems in India by selling all you own and giving the proceeds to the poor in India, your gift wouldn't make a dent in the problem, even for a day, and in the end you'd have become another candidate for a handout. No, the way some expect giving to be done is not only totally impractical; it is futile. Here Paul outlines a sane, biblical method: as God brings particular needy individuals into your purview you should help them. Not only does that make significant giving possible, it also makes it personal. Along with the gift, a witness to the gospel of Christ can be made.

And, Paul mentions that while good must be done to all men (including unbelievers), a priority must be given to helping needy Christians. That also makes sense. If Christians don't help their own, who will?

These principles and priorities should be clear in the mind of every biblical counselor. Issues arise in which he must give advice on money matters. If he is not clear about them, he will give poor, unbiblical advice.

Paul normally dictated his letters to an amanuensis and then signed them to authenticate what he had written. But here, again making this letter unusual, he says he wrote the entire letter by his own hand. And the large letters in which he ordinarily wrote (probably because of his eye disease), in this instance, lent more than enough authenticity to the letter.

One parting shot about the Judaizers (vv. 12-15). The Judaizers are motivated by fear of persecution; they are not genuine in their claims. Unlike me, says Paul, they do not preach the cross as the way of salvation because that brings down Jewish persecution on their heads. Paul knew only too well what such persecution was like (Read Acts and II Corinthians 6,11). People will act religious, tell you that they are motivated by high ideals, but underneath many are cowards. Paul had apostolic insight to read the motives of men, such as you do not. Nevertheless, you may be

13 Those who are circumcised don't keep the law themselves, but they want you to be circumcised so that they may boast about your flesh.
14 But may I never boast except about the cross of our Lord Jesus Christ, through Whom the world has been crucified to me and I to the world.
15 Neither circumcision nor uncircumcision is of any account; but what counts is a new creation.

---

certain that a number of those you counsel are motivated by personal comfort and safety, regardless of what they tell you. Knowing this, you can look for the telltale signs of it in their speech and actions.

I remember saying to a woman this last year, "From all the evidence I can gather, I can only conclude that it is money that is driving you. Am I right?" She paused and replied, "You're right; that's exactly it." Her decisions were not in harmony with her avowed purposes. There had to be inconsistency of some sort in the picture. Little comments, the plans she was making, etc., all spelled a desire to have money. In her case, a desire that was leading her to make some very foolish decisions. Knowing that this drives many, look for it. Often, as in her case, until a proper understanding of the situation is on the table where all may acknowledge and discuss it, counseling will bog down.

Having exposed the true motives of the Judaizers, Paul makes one more telling thrust: They want you to keep the law, he says, but they don't do so themselves! No sinner can keep the law. That is why Christ had to come and die. He alone kept it, satisfying all its demands, including the penalty for breaking it, so that those who trust in Him might have everlasting life. Why do you want to believe and follow hypocrites? A good point. One to make to counselees who follow inconsistent and false teachers.

What they want to do is put a few more notches on their gun handles, says Paul. They want to boast about having gotten you gentiles to submit to circumcision. They want to boast about your "flesh;" the part of your body that they want you to have removed. It is almost like the native who shrinks heads and hangs them around his belt: "See how many I slew?" That is the spirit of these people, says Paul (v. 13). But if anyone wants to boast let him join me in boasting not about how many persons I convinced to submit to circumcision; let him boast about His Lord Who died on the cross. There, alone, is something worth boasting about. By that cross the world (with all its concerns) has been put to death for me, and I to it. I live a new kind of life. You can't say that for self-salvation by circumcision!

It doesn't matter whether you are circumcised or not—that's no big

16 May peace and mercy be on all who are in line with this rule, even on God's Israel.

17 From now on let no one cause me trouble, since I bear on my body the brand-marks of Jesus.

18 May help from our Lord Jesus Christ be with your spirit, brothers. Amen.

---

deal either way. What counts is that you have been born again and are newly created in Christ Jesus to newness of life. Ah, how I wish we could get all legalistic counselees to see this! Everything focuses on the cross, and what it can do in a person's life. The true Christian life comes not from keeping legalistic rules, or from rites and ceremonies; it comes from a personal relationship to a crucified and risen Christ.

Then, the brief conclusion: I don't know how many of you agree with what I have been saying, but may mercy and peace be on all who do (v. 16). Not on those who don't! That is implied as well. How can Paul give his apostolic benediction to those who are deserting God for another gospel? How can he call down blessings on those who propagate a works-righteousness religion? There is no way possible for him to do so. Therefore, in this place (alone) Paul gives a qualified benediction to a church. Counselor, people will want you to bless their unbiblical endeavors as well. You may not do so either by tacit approval or by the very words you speak—often in prayer in a counseling session.

As a consequence of his faithful ministry, Paul has been beaten, scarred beyond measure. So, with a parting sigh he says, "I've done all I can. And I don't need any more trouble from you or those who are leading you astray. Listen to what the Lord tells you through this letter. That's it. I can't be forever straining my eyes and my body this way. It is coming apart at the seams. The broken bones, the whip lashes, the scars of every sort are evidence of my devotion to and service of Christ. They have all come from faithfully proclaiming His love and grace." Now, to those who are true brothers, may help from the Lord Jesus be given to you. Amen.

There comes a time when all has been said and done. There is nothing more that can be done by you. There is a time to tell a counselee exactly what Paul told the Galatians. I have done my best; now it is up to you to pay attention to what I have said. I call on God to bless you if you are genuine, but only if so. Remember, you can only say this convincingly if you bear the battle-marks from wounds (physical or otherwise) that you have sustained as a faithful soldier of the cross.

Introduction to
EPHESIANS

The Book of Ephesians holds a special place in the work of Christian counselors, especially for the helpful materials concerning rehabituation and communication in chapter four and the teaching about the authority/subjection spheres in chapters 5 and 6. But it is a mistake to think, therefore, that the first three chapters can be passed over as "the doctrinal section" while turning to the last three as "the practical section." As can be seen in Philippians 2, as well as elsewhere, doctrine can be applied in an exceedingly practical way. Indeed, it is my hope that after having considered the Book in some depth you will agree that the first three chapters are every bit as valuable for counseling purposes as the last three.

Despite its name, the Book of Ephesians is probably not a letter to the church of Ephesus. It is a treatise (rather than a letter) sent to the churches of Asia Minor (now Turkey), *including* the church at Ephesus. In verse one, the words "at Ephesus" are missing from the better manuscripts. There is a blank space instead, almost as if it originally read, "to the church at _____". The name of the particular church would then be filled in as a copy was sent to it. Since Ephesus was the principal church of Asia Minor, and the easiest city to reach, doubtless, it was the Ephesian manuscript that became the basis for copies sent later on to the rest of the congregations throughout the Mediterranean world. That, at least, is *one* idea of how it happened—and the most plausible.

The principal thing to understand, however, is that in Ephesians there are none of the local references we have come to expect in Paul's letters; it is not a letter but a treatise on the good ways of God with His church and the implications of these (how the church should respond). Few books, even in the more doctrinal section, could be of greater importance to the biblical counselor.

What Paul has done for us in Philippians two, we must do for ourselves in the first three chapters of Ephesians. That does not mean that there is little that is directly related to counseling as it stands; there is. But, there is also the greater possibility of applying doctrine to counseling in ways that, at first, might not be apparent. In this commentary, I shall attempt to do that only in ways that are suggestive, so that the reader may wish to go beyond in his actual use of the doctrinal materials in Chapters 1-3.

CHAPTER 1

1 Paul, an apostle of Christ Jesus by God's will to the saints who are [at Ephesus], those who are faithful in Christ Jesus:

2 May help and peace from God our Father and the Lord Jesus Christ be yours.

3 Blessed be the God and Father of our Lord Jesus Christ, Who has blessed us with every kind of spiritual blessing in the heavenly places in Christ,

---

We now study what many believe to be the greatest of the Pauline writings. He opens the letter with his official title **an apostle of Christ Jesus**. In a treatise like this, there was no place for a personal word or a warmer greeting. All sorts of people would be reading it and using it for various purposes. An apostle is a person "sent off" by another who bears all of the authority of the sender. The treatise is about the church and to the church: **to all the saints**. That is, to all who are faithful in Christ Jesus. A saint is a "set apart" person. He is one whom God Himself has called to be His own. He is, therefore, set apart from the rest of the world. Those who have genuine faith (the "faithful") constitute the lot of the saints. But notice that even this faithfulness is "in Christ Jesus." That is to say, they have and maintain faith in Him only by His mercy and grace. They can't even take credit for their faith (as he says in the next chapter; it too is the "gift" of God). Boasters beware! A Christian has a right to boast only in His Lord.

As in many of his letters, Paul wishes help and peace to rain upon his readers (v. 2). Why? Because they are the two things most "saints" can never get enough of. They need more and more of each.

Paul now launches forth on the longest sentence in the New Testament (in the original it covers the rest of the first chapter!). All modern translations break it up for better comprehension. But note, and don't miss this point, the longest sentence in the New Testament is a sentence in which Paul speaks of blessings of every kind that God has lavished upon His church (cf. v. 2). That, in itself, is a significant truth to convey to a discouraged counselee. It took the longest sentence in the Greek New Testament to describe them all. Take him to this passage and read about all that God has done for him.

According to verse 3, the blessings for which Paul expresses gratitude are **all kinds of spiritual** blessings. For these, we should praise God.

4   even as He chose us in Him before the foundation of the world to be
holy and blameless before Him. In love
5   He predestined us for adoption as His own sons through Jesus Christ
in keeping with the good pleasure of His intention,

Complaining, downcast, depressed counselees need to be reminded of all
God has done for them so that their hearts may be filled with praise and
thanksgiving. Not all Christians will receive material blessings in this life.
That they will is never promised. But spiritual blessings? Yes, of all sorts!
And they have already been given: the word "blessed [us]" is in the past
tense. They were given in Christ Jesus Who, dwelling in the heavenly
places, has poured upon us His heavenly mercy and grace. Does a counselee deny it? Then ask him to read on. The catalog of blessings that follows ought to evoke gratitude and thanksgiving from any true Christian. If
he comprehends what he reads, he will see that God has prepared for and
granted him all that he could ever possibly need (not necessarily all he
might wish).

Indeed, God the Father blessed us in Christ from the foundation of
the world because He **chose** us *to be* in Christ from before creation. And,
that choice was to bring us into His love and grace that He might make us
His holy and blameless children. That's how certain these spiritual blessings are. They were eternally determined to come to us, and, since they
were to come in Christ, they were as certain as was His coming.

Notice the first blessing: to be holy and blameless. It is possible for a
believer to become both. Certainly, neither will be complete until he, himself, reaches the heavenly places, but increasingly, he may become more
and more conformed to the One Who is entirely holy and blameless. And
that is the destiny, goal and purpose of the believer's salvation—to
become what he should be to the praise of God. Set this goal before your
counselee whose ambitions are entirely earthly. Set it before the counselee
who has given up. God never commends His children to be what He does
not provide for them to become. There is hope, then, in the aspirations of
this passage. If God wants holy, blameless saints, you can be sure He has
made that possible. Isn't that a heartening fact to hold before your counselee?!

The second spiritual blessing is the Christian's election: He **chose**
[elected] **us in Him**. It is a marvelous thing to be chosen by God. That this
choosing was before the foundation of the world makes it clear that there
is nothing of our works that has to do with that choice. Before we were

6   leading to the praise of His glorious grace, which He presented to us as a gift in the beloved One.

---

born, before there was a world, God had chosen a group of people as His very own. The choice was purely out of grace. In no sense was human merit involved. There is great assurance and certainty in this fact. Once a person is saved, how could he ever be lost? God has ordained from before the foundation of the world that he will belong to Him! One's salvation is certain. If it was certain before there was a human being created (as Paul says it was), the question is Who made it certain? And the answer is absolutely clear: the only Being in existence: God. God made your election secure by planning it before time began. That should be reassuring for doubting, wondering Christians who are unsure of whether salvation lasts.

It was **in love** that God **predestined** believers for **adoption**; the next spiritual blessing. People who believe the Bible must believe in predestination; it is taught again and again on its pages. Here we encounter the term. It is the preordained plan of God, according to His purpose to show love to poor sinners, choosing some to become saints whom He adopts into His family. The concept of adoption was well-defined in the Roman world. Even emperors of Rome adopted those they chose to follow them so that they would receive the rights and privileges of sonship. The word "adopt" is, at once, a warm and a legal term. It means, literally, "child-placing," and has to do with placing or "setting" a child in a family. It also means that one receives a new name, an inheritance, full rights and privileges of family members, etc. The adopted child is no different from a birth-child, except that it was chosen and brought into the family as an act of love. God, in love, didn't determine to make slaves of those He chose but sons. Predestination is often thought of as a cold, lifeless doctrine. It is anything but. Here Paul describes it as a act of love on God's part. And, this adoption, determined from all eternity, was **in keeping with the good pleasure of His intention**. That is, it happened just as He intended it to happen; there was no slip-up in the execution of His plan. And what He intended was solely His proactive intention; no one had any influence on His decisions in the matter. He planned what He would do, and He did exactly what He planned to do. Explain this to counselees and bid them take heart.

And, he did this ultimately **to the praise of His glorious grace**. Without a doubt whatever God plans and does redounds to His honor. He planned that the choice and redemption of a people who would become

> **7** In Him we have redemption through His blood, the forgiveness of trespasses, in keeping with the riches of His grace

His sons, adopted into the full privileges of His family, would honor Him by displaying the glory of His grace. Grace is not only unmerited favor; rather, it is favor shown to one who deserves the opposite. God's amazing love in saving some, while satisfying His own justice, despite their sin, is a remarkable thing. He could not simply allow them to sin and turn His back. So He sent His Son to shed His blood, dying on the cross in the place of guilty sinners who, believing in Him, might be forgiven as, in grace, He also satisfied the claims of the law on their behalf. Your counselee's job description is to display, before the universe, how glorious God's grace is by exhibiting its fruits in his life.

And, this grace was presented to us believers **as a gift** in the beloved One (v. 6). This is the crux of the matter. All these spiritual blessings, coming to us in such profusion, are a gift. We didn't earn them; God simply supplied them. Proud counselees, thinking that they deserve something, would do well to consider the teaching in this chapter: all is of grace. If a believer does anything worthwhile, it is only because God chose Him to do that very thing and made it possible for him to do it. He has nothing to be proud of. Except Christ, Who did it all for Him. When disheartened Christians come to see you, remind them of their adoption. If you are counseling people who have forgotten the glories of the cross, then, here is the place to help them remember. Read, marvel, give thanks!

As a matter of fact, it might not be a bad idea to begin a second or third counseling session with the reading of this first chapter. It should set the atmosphere for much of what you have to do and say in the sessions to come. And, it will be present to everyone's mind if you need to refer other's to it.

These first six verses say it all, but Paul is not satisfied to say it one way only. He comes at the matter of God's undeserved goodness to His church again and again from various perspectives. That, in fact, is what we encounter in verses 7ff. The choice, the adoption, the love of God shown to us in Christ was what was effected in our redemption and the forgiveness of our trespasses. These theological concepts are so commonly known and understood, I do not want to spend time on them. (See the exegetical commentaries.) But, notice, the blessings are **in keeping with the riches of His grace**. That means, among other things, that this grace that redeemed and forgave us and which was "lavished on us" (v. 8)

8   that He lavished on us. With all wisdom and understanding
9   He made known to us the secret of His intention that is in keeping with
His good pleasure that He purposed in Christ,
10   regarding an arrangement that will bring the seasons to their fulfillment by heading up all things again in Christ, things in the heavens and
things on the earth.

---

is not all the grace available. There is a rich store of grace possessed by
the Father, which He gives to His own (cf. v. 2). There is grace for times
of trouble, there is grace to overcome one's anger, there is grace to put lust
and adulterous life-styles away for good. Indeed, there is more than
enough grace for every need the believer may have. When a counselee
complains, "I don't know if I can find it in me to go on" tell him that is not
the problem. We know that there is not strength and wisdom in him; the
question is whether there is help to go on from an outside source. And
here is Paul's answer—there is plenty of help available from the store-
house where God has amassed riches of grace. And, they are as available
to your counselee in Christ as they are to Christ Himself. What then is his
complaint? Turn to the proper source and there can be no problem. If the
problem persists, somehow he is failing to avail himself of all that God
has provided. Probe what he is doing to find out how. As a child of God,
the Father's wealth of grace is available. And, notice, this isn't something
for which counselees must beg. These blessings have been provided
already in Christ Jesus.

But there is more. These spiritual blessings include **all sorts of wisdom and understanding** (v. 8). Precisely what most counselees need:
understanding of God's will, understanding of the situation. Wisdom to
know what to do in delicate circumstances, wisdom to make decisions and
plans. In Christ, from before time began, God determined to give these
things to his adopted sons. How, then, can believers claim they do not
have the wisdom and understanding in any given situation to do the right
thing? They have both—in God's Word—if only they will read and use
what God prescribes therein. The Christian ought to be the sharpest person in his community. After all, look at the foundation of truth he stands
upon. He understands life, the purpose of it, the future of it, etc. Who else
does? He has God as His Father, and, in Christ, all the riches of wisdom
and understanding He wishes to impart. What a shame it is, then, to see
Christians defeated, perplexed, failing to use the spiritual blessings with
which they have been endowed!

11 In Him we were chosen as His inheritance, being predestined according to the purpose of the One Who is operating everything in agreement with the counsel of His will,
12 so that we may be the praise of His glory—we who previously hoped in Christ.

God, then, has made His great plan of redemption known to His people (v. 9), a redemption that was somewhat obscure in the Old Testament era, and that only came into full light after the cross and resurrection. The mystery has been cleared up. This is God's plan to bring all things under subjection to Christ. As the seasons He ordained are fulfilled, and His plan is completed, everything in heaven and earth is to be subjected to Jesus, who will be Head of the universe (cf. v. 22). Think of it! You are a son of God and a fellow-heir with Jesus Christ. You are involved in this glorious plan of God that is bringing about the exaltation of His Son. He graciously disclosed this plan to you, so that you would know all that He has done for you and all He has made available to you. That is another blessing—that God would confide in you what He is doing (vv. 9,10). Life is not without meaning!

In verses 11-14 Paul continues to recite the blessings of God's grace to the members of His church. In Christ, He (God, the Father) has chosen us to be His (Christ's) inheritance. And He (the Father) predestinated us according to His own purposes—the purposes of the One Who operates **everything in agreement with the counsel of His own will**. Now there is a reassuring statement if there ever was one. Some counselees complain that the world is against them, everything is going wrong, that there is no fairness in life, and what not. Read this verse to them. From God's perspective, everything is going exactly as it should. And if they would only bring their perspective into agreement with Gods' there would be no reason for complaint. In many ways we all need to adjust to God's purposes. His timetable is not the same as ours; we want things to happen now. He is willing to wait until all that He has in mind is accomplished. We, then, must learn patience. Our perspective is so narrow and limited in both space and time that we cannot begin to understand the ways of God in this world, but we can believe what Paul writes in verse 11, and rejoice in what comes to pass. It is not necessary for us to know all of the purposes of God in order to have the faith that He is doing all things well on behalf of Christ's church. We must simply look at what He has done through the ages, in our lives individually, etc., to understand and believe.

13 In Him you too, by hearing the Word of truth—the good news of your salvation—when you also believed in Him, were sealed with the promised Holy Spirit,

14 Who is the down payment on our inheritance until the redemption that allows us to take possession of it, for the praise of His glory.

We—the early converts to Christ's church (perhaps, Jews), says Paul, those who previously put their hope (expectation) in Christ—exist not for our own sakes, but to praise and honor the One Who chose and predestined us to glory (v. 12). Paul includes himself in that number. But he sees the very same purpose and blessings for those to whom he is writing (perhaps gentiles), who later trusted the Savior: **In Him you too...** (v. 13[a]). Like us, says Paul, you too were sealed with the promised Holy Spirit (John the Baptist and Jesus had both promised His coming) Who entered into your life when you believed the gospel that you heard preached to you. This sealing by the Spirit is like the down payment on our inheritance that we retain until the day when we take full possession of it. When I was a boy, dad made a down payment on a wagon, but I didn't take it home right away—as you do now. No. Each week dad paid something on the wagon until the whole was paid. Then I got it. In the meanwhile, the wagon stayed in the store. But, so that no one else could buy it, a tag with my father's name was tied to it. That tag served the same purpose as the "seal" in our text. The tag or seal identifies the owner of the item tagged or sealed. Now, of course, the analogy breaks down at the point where payment comes in; but that is not what Paul wants to emphasize. His concern is to observe that though God has paid the full price by Christ's blood, only when He redeems His children will the possession of the inheritance be ours. The figure is a bit mixed, since it is the believer who is sealed, rather than the inheritance. But the point is that we are as surely His as if we had been redeemed, taken from the store and given the inheritance. How do we know this? Because we have God's own self—the Holy Spirit—to mark us out as His own who will at length enter into the heavenly inheritance.

Show your counselee that it is enough to have God's seal. Often one gets itchy for the inheritance. You want to leave the trouble and problems of this world behind. But there is work here to do. Yet, if you have the tag of God hanging from you, that is all you need. Ask, "Have you seen the fruit of the Spirit in your life (I didn't say in great profusion), but have you tasted a grape or two)? Then you are His child, destined for the heav-

73

15 For this reason, I too, hearing about the faith in the Lord Jesus that is among you, and about your love for all of the saints,

16 never cease to give thanks for you, mentioning you in my prayers,

17 that the God of our Lord Jesus Christ, the glorious Father, may give you a spirit of wisdom and of revelation in a full knowledge of Him,

---

enly inheritance." Be prepared to discuss the fact that the redemption day when God comes to claim him as His own is in His hands, and that now it is his task to live for God until that day, all the while rejoicing because he is sealed with His mark!

Now comes Paul's thanksgiving and prayer. Though Paul has a particular group of churches in mind, there are none of the particular notices that we find in letters addressed to specific churches. He has heard good things in general about the churches in Asia Minor. He understands that there is strong faith and love manifested by them (v. 15). And, for that he continually gives thanks to God as he prays for them (v. 16). What he prays, is for even more blessings to come the way of the members of Christ's church (vv. 17-21). It is amazing to recount all that God does for the believer immediately, and then to realize there is much more that He showers down upon him from day to day. For these ongoing blessings he prays.

But, specifically, for what does he pray? First, that God out of His glorious riches will grant a spirit of wisdom and of revelation so that your counselee may have a full knowledge of Christ. Your counselee is perplexed? He doesn't know which way to turn? Join him in praying that he may become wise. But note that the wisdom and the revelation of truth pertain to a knowledge of Jesus Christ. God's gives answers to particular problems not so much by the laying down of rules but by giving a closer, more intimate knowledge of His Son in Whom are all the treasure of wisdom and knowledge. Tell your counselee, "You may be praying for wisdom to make a decision; good. But don't be surprised if God gives you a fuller knowledge of Christ as the answer. When you know Him better, you will become more like Him, able to act wisely in ways that are pleasing to God because, like Him, you will know how to depend on, interpret and implement the Scriptures better (v. 17)."

Assure him by reminding him that "Christ called you. But you need more and more to understand the nature and purpose of that calling. What it involves; what He expects of you. So, Paul prays that the eyes of your heart (the thinking and decision-making element in you) may be enlight-

18 enlightening the eyes of your heart so that you may know what the hope of His calling is, what the riches of His glorious inheritance for the saints are,
19 and what the immeasurable greatness of His power for us who believe is. It is in keeping with the force of His mighty strength
20 that He exerted for Christ when He raised Him from the dead, and seated Him in the heavenly places at His right hand,
21 far above all rule and authority and power and lordship, and every name that is named not only in this age, but also in the coming one.

---

ened to do so. He wants you to know what to **expect** (the meaning of the word hope in the Bible) from this calling." That, of course, is what is wrong with many counselees. They do not have biblical expectations in regard to their lives and in regard to the faith. They need to know what to expect. If they have been sold a bed-of-roses Christianity, they need to know that this was wrong; that faith involves suffering, even persecution. If they expected that trusting Christ would clear up all difficulties in their lives, but now, they seem only to have greater ones, they need to understand that Christianity places on them the responsibility to exercise greater care in living and, consequently, the necessity for more cautious decision-making than ever before. Until one becomes accustomed to it, this change may complicate life. Pray that as you explain proper expectations to them, countering the errors they think and live by, that God will truly **enlighten** their hearts.

Every counselee needs to understand how great God's power is, and that this omnipotent power is **for us who believe** (v. 19). How great is the power of God that is available to meet the problems of life? The power God provided for you to live for Him is the same power that God used to raise His Son from the dead (and you want to turn to Freud?)! It is a power greater than anything the evil one can throw at you. Telling the counselee this, enabling him to understand and to draw upon this power by the reading and living of Scripture in answer to prayer, is one of the principal tasks a biblical counselor performs. He is enabling the counselee to depend on God and Christ rather than on himself or on the counselor. He is also removing all excuse-making.

Thinking of Christ's resurrection, Paul goes on to speak of How He was exalted to the Father's right hand (v. 20) far above all authority and power on the earth or in the heavens. He is supreme (v. 21). And, what is He doing in that place of authority? How does he exercise it? He is ruling over all things **for the sake of His church** (v. 22)! So, the power and

75

22 He has subjected everything under His feet, made Him Head over all things for the sake of the church,
23 which is His body, the fullness of Him Who fills everything every-where.

---

authority of Christ are being exerted in behalf of your Christian coun-selee. How important it is for him to come to that conviction. He has con-stituted the Church as His body, through which He fully works everywhere to do everything He does. Christ will use him for His glory. That is what a counselee needs to hear. Again, the true expectation of one's calling is essential.

CHAPTER 2

1 Now you were dead in your trespasses and sins,

2   in which you once walked in agreement with the world's ways, in accord with the ruler who has the authority of the air, the spirit who is now at work in the sons of disobedience,

---

Having laid out the blessings that God's redemption provides for His church, Paul now proceeds to examine in more detail just how He effected salvation. In a very powerful way, he explains how God can remain just while justifying guilty sinners. What he teaches is important not only to theologians and Bible students, it has large implications for one's counseling practices as well.

He begins with the remarkable statement that human beings were born **dead**. Death, of course, is *separation*. When the spirit is separated from the body, physical death occurs. When the spirit is separated from God, spiritual death occurs. When the spirit and the body are both separated from God, eternal death (the second death) occurs. Here, Paul is speaking of spiritual death. Often, for one reason or another, counselees must be instructed about this basic theological truth as well as those that follow. Error, or lack of understanding, may be part of the problem.

People are born dead to God. That is a significant statement. It means that just as if you went down to the local cemetery to counsel those bodies in the graves and you would get absolutely no response, so too when you counsel those who are *dead* "in trespasses and sins" you will receive no response. In a number of places, including comments on I Corinthians 2, I have written clearly about the futility (not to say harm) of attempting to counsel unbelievers. It is impossible to get them to make changes in their lives that please God (Cf. Romans 8:8). If they change at all, it will be from one life-style that displeases God to another that equally does so. And God has not called you to help people to adopt ways that do not glorify Him. The counselor becomes a counselor only when it is possible to help a counselee make changes that are in accord with the will of God. Prior to that time, he should refuse to counsel; he must evangelize unbelievers, just as God has told him to.

So, until something happens to him to give him spiritual life, the sinner is dead spiritually. That means he is unresponsive to the things of God's Spirit that are found in Scripture (Again, see comments on I Corinthians 2). But, Paul says (vv. 4,5), in mercy, God gave Christians spiritual

3   among whom also we all once lived our lives by following the desires of our flesh, doing what the flesh and the impulses want. So, by nature, we too were children of wrath, just like the rest.

---

life (he **made us alive**). The initiative had to come from God; it could not come from dead persons. There is neither desire nor ability on the part of the spiritually dead to respond to the teachings of God; they are impervious to them. Take an unbeliever to a church service and he will tell you, "Boy, that was a dead meeting!" It may have been the most wonderful preaching in the world, but not to him. In reality, it is not the meeting that was dead, *he* was dead to it. So, until God first does the work of giving life to the unbeliever, to enable him to respond in faith and obedience, it is futile to attempt to get him to make changes that conform to the Bible. To the extent that he is able to do so, changes will only be outward, and those changes will be superficial. There will be no inner change at all. You will have helped him only to move dangerously close to the hypocrites that Christ condemned so severely. He is likely to become a whited sepulcher or a proud cup washed on the outside, but full of corruption within.

Now, before God gives spiritual life (that is, regenerates those He has chosen to become His sons in Christ), the chosen ones are just like others who have not been destined to eternal life: Paul says they are **just like the rest** (v. 3ᶜ). By nature, they are oriented away from God and toward self-serving interests. They **walked** (*walk* is the biblical word for a life-style, a pattern of life) **according to the ways of the world** (v. 2). They thought like unbelievers, they acted like unbelievers, they talked like unbelievers because they *were* unbelievers! They were born children of the evil one (v. 2). They were in accord with all his ways (v. 2). He is that spirit who is now at work in the **sons of disobedience** (unbelievers, whose lives are characterized by disobedience to God). He is the devil, whose realm, like the air, penetrates into all parts of this world, into every nook and cranny (Cf. I John 5:19). If he is a son of disobedience, like his father, the devil, he will not comply with the teachings of Scripture. Any attempted efforts to get him to do so are futile. Like father, like son—his natural orientation is to disobey God.

This sinful, God-rejecting nature with which we all come into this world, encourages us to follow **the desires of the flesh** (the body, wrongly habituated), acting and living according to its impulses (dominant feelings of the moment). The unbeliever, no matter how much he tells you otherwise, is a feeling-oriented, feeling-motivated person.

4   But God, Who is rich in mercy, because of His great love with which
He loved us,
5   even when we were dead in trespasses, made us alive together with
Christ (by grace you have been saved),
6   and raised us up with Him, and seated us with Him in the heavenly
places, in Christ Jesus,

Beneath his seemingly, cool, logical exterior, you will find someone who
is living according to his desires and impulses. Mention Christian teaching about predestination and election to him, for instance, and you will
almost always receive a strong, negative, *emotional* response. Tell Him
Christ is the only way to salvation and watch him hit the ceiling. Moreover, in his positive responses, watch him jostle and grab (often in subtle
ways, of course) for whatever he can to satisfy the desires of self. And, it
is these ways of life that have become habituated into his thinking and
behavior that, when he is converted, come along with him. They are not
automatically shed at regeneration. Rather, they become a problem for
him in attempting now to become a son of *obedience*. And it is with these
habitual ways that the Christian counselor finds himself deeply involved
in counseling. Be aware that God here defines non-Christian living as
desire and emotion-oriented living. Look for such patterns in your counselee, remembering that they often lay beneath a cool exterior. But more
of this in chapter 4.

By nature, the chosen ones were **children of wrath**. What does that
mean? Well, just like the rest, they too deserved hell, where those who do
not trust Christ will experience the ultimate wrath of God throughout eternity. But for the love of God extended to them in great mercy, like the rest
of mankind, they too would suffer that wrath (v. 3). But God's love, out of
pure mercy and grace, was shown toward His chosen ones, and He provided a way in which their guilt could be dealt with, without they, themselves, having to bear the punishment of eternal wrath. That is the good
news of salvation in Jesus Christ. He took their punishment, their hell, for
them. They are counted to have died with Christ and risen with Him to
newness of life, a heavenly life like the life of the Savior with Whom
believers also are counted to be seated already in heavenly places (v. 6).

It is the task of the counselor to work with counselees so as to help
them to live lives that no longer accord with the world's ways, but with
heavenly ways. That is a function of sanctification—something possible
only in the lives of the regenerate. It is worth noting, then, that counseling

7   in order that for ages to come He might demonstrate the immeasurable riches of His grace, by showing kindness toward us in Christ Jesus.

8 By grace you have been saved through faith and this is not from you (it is the gift of God).

9   nor is it from works, lest anyone should boast.

---

is a ministry of the Word to the regenerate; a means of sanctification (setting them apart more and more from sinful ways to righteous ones).

Why has God done this? Why has His love been so generously lavished on undeserving sinners? What motivated grace? Nothing within the person receiving the mercy; that is certain. According to verse 7, in redemption, God wished to demonstrate an aspect of his nature. He wanted to demonstrate **the riches of His grace**. But, if there had been no sinners, deserving of hell, that side of His nature could never have been demonstrated to the universe. So, because He wished to do so, God arranged matters in a way that made men alone responsible for their sin. Then, in His grace, out of love, it was possible for God to redeem them. Thus, He could demonstrate His mercy and grace (cf. my book, *The Grand Demonstration*, for a full discussion of the demonstration of God's wrath as well as His mercy).

But, precisely, how does redemption occur? The elect are saved by God's **grace** *through faith*. This salvation from sin and its penalties, as well as the faith through which it is appropriated, is **the gift of God** (v. 8). In other words, from start to finish, it is God who saves. There is nothing of human works involved (v. 9). For that we can be eternally grateful; wherever salvation would have depended on human works it would have failed. Salvation is secured to God's chosen ones because it is a salvation conceived and accomplished by God Himself. The sinful works of man cannot produce the righteousness of God.

But there is another reason that salvation is not of works: God wants no one to be able to **boast**. When a redeemed sinner gets to heaven, he will not be able to say "It is because of ME." Nor will he be able to put his arm around Jesus and say, "WE" did it. He will point away from himself to the Lord Jesus Christ and say, "HE." God wants no one to boast (v. 9). That fact, of course, as I have already observed is significant. The counselor who detects boasting and pride in his counselee, needs to help him eliminate it. Pride goes before a fall (in the case of some counselees, it is the cause of a fall that they have already experienced!). Plainly, God has said He wants no boasting. And here is one way to do eliminate boasting.

10 Indeed, we are His handiwork, created in Christ Jesus for good works that God prepared before hand so that we might walk in them.

Remind him of these verses in which God says that it was He Who raised him from spiritual death, gave him life and provided faith for him to believe the gospel. Where then is his reason to boast? It was all of God. If it had not been for His initiative, there would have been no change; he would have gone on serving **the prince of the power of the air**.

Indeed, as Paul goes on to say, **we are His handiwork**. We are on display as the products of God's hands. He has brought about our salvation; it is to Him that every one of us should look with gratitude for anything worthwhile that may be found in our lives. And the purpose of this workmanship by God is, through Jesus, to enable us to perform those good works that God, long ago, prepared for us to do (v. 10). These works constitute an entirely different life-style (or walk). But where do we get these good works? Do we begin with grace, but end with human effort? No. These good works are **prepared beforehand** by God Himself. We do not need to decide which works are good and which are not; He has determined that and told us in His Word. We have a divine standard that distinguishes good from evil. We do not have to guess. Nor do we have to stir up some power within in order to accomplish them; it is the Spirit Who enables us to perform them. They are His fruit (see Galatians 5). So, even the works that we do, as the result of regeneration, we do by the wisdom and power of God. Therefore, you can see that everything, from beginning to end, is the fruit of God's grace.

Since God's purpose in creating us anew in Christ is to have us do good works and glorify our Father that is in heaven, in effect, the calling of the counselor is to help counselees to discover what these good works are and to teach him how to accomplish them. In the fourth chapter, where Paul enlarges on the change of life-style that God desires, we shall see how he uses the counselor to assist in the process.

Paul now considers the matter of this new creation in Christ as it relates to the church. Mankind was created as one. Sin entered and, with it, division. Part of that division was between Jews and Gentiles—something that never would have come about had it not been for Adam's sin. God was introducing the Savior of *all* through a *part*. But, in the new creation that takes place through God's handiwork, there is no longer any division. The Savior has come out of the seed of Abraham and, now, all who believe in Him are spiritual children of Abraham *by their faith*. This

11 Therefore, remember that at one time you Gentiles by flesh, who are called "the uncircumcision" by those who are called "the circumcision" (which is done to the flesh by human hands)—

12 remember that at that time you were apart from Christ, aliens who had no right of citizenship in Israel, and strangers from the covenants with their promises, having no hope and no God in the world.

13 But now in Christ Jesus, you who once were far off have come near by the blood of Christ.

14 He is our peace, Who made both of us one, and has torn down the wall of enmity between us that divided us,

---

new state of things was a matter that needed discussion, since there was much confusion and wrong thinking about it. Paul takes the time to clear up difficulties. He recalls that at one time, these gentiles to whom he was writing, were called the "**uncircumcision**" by those who called themselves the "**circumcision**" (v. 11). He reminds them that, at that time, they were apart from Christ, aliens, without citizenship in God's covenant community of Israel, **strangers from the promises** God gave that community, and without any expectation of a future, because they did not know the true God (v. 12). But now this sorry state has changed. Since they trusted in Christ, though they were previously **far off**, they have now **come nea**r to God (v. 13). Through His shed blood, by dying in their place, Christ made them God's children, citizens of the heavenly country. That is why they should live a life in accord with heavenly values and standards. That means more than the currently undefined (and undefinable) concept of "Family Values."

Verse 14 clearly defines the church as one entity. Any dissension between Jews and gentiles that may have persisted before, in Christ, has been dissolved. He has brought **peace**. He has torn down **the middle wall of partition** that existed, causing **enmity** and division. This wall divided the court of the gentiles from the inner, holy areas in the temple. There was a sign (excavated by archeologists in 1871) that forbade gentiles from passing beyond this wall upon pain of death. It is to that wall, and all that wall stood for (symbolized by the sign it bore) that Paul was alluding here. In other words, in Christ's Church, there is no such division. All may worship God on the very same basis.

The Old Testament regulations that required separation between Jews and Gentiles were, by the death of Christ, abolished forever, so that from the two, God might create **a new man**—the Christian. That was the "peace" He achieved, a peace dearly purchased by the blood of Jesus.

15 by abolishing in His flesh the law of commandments with its regulations, so that from the two He might create in Himself one new man,
thereby making peace,
16 and that in one body He might reconcile both to God by the cross, putting the enmity to death in it.
17 **He came and preached peace to you who were far off and peace to
those who were near;**
18 through Him we both have access to the Father by one Spirit.
19 So then you are no longer strangers and aliens, but rather you are citizens together with the saints and members of God's household,

---

Now the regulations given by way of commandments about food, dress
and a dozen or so other things that separated the Jews from the gentiles
was abolished in Christ. Sometimes people are unaware of what in the
Old Testament is abolished and what is not. It was not only the sacrificial
system, which prefigured the coming Savior, that was no longer needed
because the final sacrifice had been made, but all those ordinances that
separated the Jew from the Gentile which (as Paul here states) are also no
longer needed.

On the cross (v. 16) Jesus put the enmity between Jew and Gentile to
death. From that time on, the two are reconciled so as to form not two, but
one body, the Church. Christ came into this world and preached (personally, and through His apostolic representatives) this peace to both the
Gentiles, who were **far off** and to the Jews, who were **near**. And, equally,
now they both have access to the same heavenly Father by the one Spirit
Who dwells in both.

So, says Paul, you Gentiles no longer are **strangers and aliens**, but,
together with the Jews who believe, you are saints of God, citizens of
heaven, and members of His **household** (v. 19). Then, taking his cue from
the word "household," which was close to the word "house," (the word for
"temple") he thinks of the church itself as a **building** (vv. 20-22) that is
built on the **foundation of the apostles and prophets**. That is to say, at its
beginning, the founding of the Church's congregations and its divine revelation came from apostles and prophets (men like Mark and Luke who,
though not apostles, nevertheless were recipients of revelation—see 3:5).
But apostles and prophets, like the foundation of any building, come *first*.
The foundation being laid, there is no longer need for more of it. The
walls and roof are not foundation. So, too, the foundation-laying process
of apostolic and prophetic activity ceased with the death of those who
were called to engage in the process. There is no revelation or apostolic

20 built on the foundation of the apostles and prophets, with Christ Jesus Himself as the chief Cornerstone.
21 In Him the whole building being fitted together grows into a holy temple in the Lord.

---

authority in the church today except as it is found in the Scriptures of the New Testament.

It is important when dealing with counselees who believe they are receiving revelation through dreams, visions, etc., to make it clear that that was all foundational activity, which has ceased. This passage, in conjunction with 3:5, should prove useful for such purposes (cf. II Corinthians 12:12). Of course, if the supposed revelations are the result of bodily chemistry gone awry through drugs, sleep loss, etc., then, another approach is necessary.

Extending the metaphor of the building, Paul continues, likening the Church to a building not only built on the apostles and prophets, but on Jesus Christ as the **chief cornerstone**—the stone from which all else was figured; He is the One to Whom the rest of the building is oriented and fitted, so that it is **growing into a temple for the Lord**. In it Paul contemplates God dwelling by His Spirit (vv. 21,22). It is instructive that God would **dwell** in a church that is composed of stones which were once Jew or Gentile, but are now not so distinguished. That was the *new* thing about which there could be no question if God Himself designed such a house.

Now, we could take off on all sorts of angles from this discussion by Paul. But only one seems to be of most importance—the absolute equality of all before God in His church. No regulations or restrictions ought to be made that hinder anyone because of his background from entering into all those activities and privileges of Christ's church. Ethnic congregations, for instance, are not the ideal and should be discouraged. There are no second class citizens of the empire of God. Often, this issue will come before the counselor. He is provided with infallible directions about the matter in Ephesians 2.

Of course, normal functional distinctions remain. Husbands as over against wives, children as over against parents, etc., have roles that will be clearly distinguished *in this very letter*. Personal qualifications that distinguish those eligible for the eldership or diaconate from those who are not, are retained and affirmed by Paul in I Timothy and Titus. But equal status of all members of Christ's church *before God*, must be maintained. Counselors often encounter attitudes and practices in counselees that violate

22 In Him you also are being built together into a place for God to dwell by His Spirit.

---

these clear teachings of the Scriptures. When you do, why not point out that any one who is being wrongly discriminated against is like one wrongly rejecting a stone that God Himself has quarried for the building He calls the church and that, if He is satisfied to dwell in that building, so too should every Christian? And, it is the counselor's obligation and privilege to hammer and chisel in order to make stones fit one another. Indeed, every counselor should see himself as a stone mason!

CHAPTER 3

1 For this reason, I Paul, the prisoner of Christ Jesus for the sake of you Gentiles—
2 if indeed you heard about the stewardship of God's grace that was given to me for you,
3 how by revelation the secret was made known to me, even as I wrote you briefly before.

In chapter three, Paul further discusses the problem of the Gentile and the Jew in the Church of Christ. The emphasis is on the Gentiles, the very sort of people to whom he was writing. He begins by saying that he is **a prisoner for the sake of** the Gentiles to whom he is writing (v. 1). How is that? He says, you would understand this if, indeed, you heard about the **stewardship of the grace of God that was given to me** for the Gentiles. He is referring to the divine commission following his conversion experience on the Damascus road (Cf. Acts 9:15), which was acknowledged at the meeting in Jerusalem by the apostles (Galatians 2:7-9). Paul was, *par excellence*, the apostle to the Gentiles.

It is interesting to note that Paul acknowledged the limitations on his stewardship, and could spell them out as he did here. That meant, first of all, that he knew what tasks God had given to him to perform as His steward. It was a stewardship of **grace** (not of works) that he dispensed through the preaching of the gospel. Secondly, he knew it was a **stewardship**. A stewardship is a trust committed by one who owns something to another who administers it for him. Paul was the steward of God's marvelous grace that he was the minister to **the Gentiles**.

Every biblical counselor is also a steward. There is no way he can claim credit for what he dispenses. Or for the ministry he exercises. As he ministers the Scriptures, he should recognize that all that is worthwhile to give is but what God has first given to him. He must see himself as *nothing more* than a steward. Too often, because of the power granted a counselor by counselees, he may begin to think of himself as the *source* of wisdom and authority. If he does, he has left his ministry and has become a free agent on his own. Those who operate outside the church are particularly tempted to do that very thing. The very setting and seeming autonomy of that context contributes greatly to the temptation. There is only one thing required of a steward: that he is found to be **faithful** (I Corinthians 4:2). That is precisely what is at stake.

4   By referring to and reading it you can make a judgment about my understanding of the secret of Christ
5   which was not made known to human beings in other generations as it now has been revealed to His holy apostles and prophets by the Spirit,

---

Now, that the Gentiles were to become a part of God's Church on an equal footing with the Jews, that was something not widely understood. There were hints, of course, in the promise to Abraham, and in some of the Psalms and the prophets, but as the Jews thought about this, they thought that the Gentiles would be blessed by first becoming Jews. That, however, was not how God was doing things. In verse 3, Paul says that the secret (a **mystery** in Scripture is something that has not yet been revealed, but will be, and is best translated **secret or open secret**; it is not something mysterious) was made known to him. The way in which God was going to include the Gentiles was made known to him **by revelation** (thus the idea of *open* secret). This, he had taught plainly, in a shorter letter (v. 3).

Revelation is divinely-given data. It is communicated directly to a prophet or apostle, or to him through another prophet who received it directly from God. Because the truth about this matter was given by revelation, it could not be wrong. Paul is defining the nature of the authority that stands behind what he is about to teach. If you have any further questions about this, says Paul, I refer you to my previous letter. Compare and contrast it with what I am now about to say, and you can make your own judgment about my interpretation of this matter (v. 4). Here is what he says:

"This truth about the Gentiles was not understood as clearly in past **generations**, but now it is an open secret since all the **apostles and prophets** of this New Testament era have had a revelation about it. I am not alone in this matter." Notice, in passing, that the apostolic and the prophetic offices, which were temporary since they were given for laying the *foundation* of the Church (see 2:20), were *revelatory offices*. With the completion of the foundation, and the passing of these offices, revelation also disappeared. Revelation from the Spirit was necessary until such a time as it was complete and could be gathered together in the Book we call the New Testament. But, it was foundational only. Everything since, rests on that secure foundation. The Spirit continues to work through that same revelation. He reveals nothing new, but He is actively applying what He once revealed long ago to modern problems that counselees present.

6   that is, that the Gentiles are to be joint heirs, united in one body and sharers of the promise in Christ Jesus through the good news

7   of which I became a servant by the gift of God's grace that was given to me by the working of His power.

8   To me, the very least of all saints, this grace was given to announce to the Gentiles the good news of the inexhaustible riches of Christ,

9   and to bring to light what the arrangement of the secret that for ages was hidden by God, the Creator of all things, is like.

That is why the Scriptures are necessary in counseling.

But what is the secret, now disclosed by revelation? Verse 6 says it all: the Gentiles were to be **joint heirs** with the Jews, **united into one body with them and sharers of all the promises** made to them. All this comes through the **gospel** of Jesus Christ (not through ceremonies or works of the law).

In the seventh verse, Paul says he became a **servant** of this good news. That is to say, his ministry consisted of the proclamation of the gospel. And, he received his call to the work out of **grace** (certainly not of merit; he had persecuted the Church), as a **gift** from God. God's **power** converted him and turned him into an apostle. Nothing short of the exercise of that sort of power could have turned him around. Paul is amazed that God called him. He never lost this sense of astonishment. In verse 8 you hear it as he writes of being the **very least of all saints**.

And, unlike a salesman who works for money only, he dearly appreciates the product that he sells. Listen to him describe it as Christ's **inexhaustible riches**. And that is no hype, no sales talk; it is his honest opinion about what he has to offer freely, without money and without price. Though by now all the apostles and prophets understood the secret, Paul, as the apostle to the Gentiles, was given the special task of **announcing** this fact throughout the world and the Church (cf. v. 8, "to me"). And, as a part of that proclamation, he was able to **bring to light** how God had **arranged** what He had kept secret from the beginning, and that was hidden for a time. Paul was able to explain what that arrangement was all about; how from creation God arranged things so that the Gentiles could come into the Church on the same footing as the Jews.

And, God did things this way so that His **many-sided wisdom** (which Paul was privy to by revelation) could be displayed by Christ's Church before heavenly beings. Once again we have the emphasis of the universe looking on in wonder at what God is doing in this planet for poor, sinful human beings. To remember that you are a part of a divine

10 This was so that God's many-sided wisdom might now be made known by the church to the rulers and to the authorities in the heavenly places

11 in agreement with the eternal purpose that He accomplished by Christ Jesus our Lord,

12 in Whom we have boldness and confidence of access through faith in Him.

13 So, I ask you not to become discouraged over the afflictions that I am suffering for you because these are your glory.

14 For this reason (I say), I bend my knees to the Father

---

drama that is being enacted for others is important. And, it is equally important for your counselee to know this. When counselees say, "It's my life and I'll live it as I please," you may counter with the fact that his life is on public display before the *universe*.

God had planned from eternity to display his wisdom, grace and mercy before other beings that He created (v. 11) by demonstrating the accomplishments of Jesus Christ that are exhibited in His Church. In Christ, we have learned that we need not stand far off from God; we may have boldness and confidence, says Paul, to approach Him through faith. Counselees, afraid of God, must be directed to a verse like this. That is precisely what they need to know—they can come boldly before the throne of Grace to find help in time of need. Paul certainly availed himself of this free access (note the "we"). So should you, as you are careful never to forget that counseling, in the most basic sense, is an element of the grand demonstration of God's mercy and grace.

Paul's point: "Since we both have equal access to God, don't become discouraged (or "give up"), he says, because I am suffering in prison. These sufferings ought to be your glory (v. 13)." What does he mean by that? Simply this: that by God's grace he was able to proclaim the gospel to them, that led to opposition and **sufferings**. Those sufferings are but a sign of God's goodness, a trophy of His grace. It was a glorious task to which he had been called. They should **glory** in it with him.

Because Paul gloried in tribulation, he says, he bows his knees to God. In all his suffering, you must help your counselee to see that the reason to come to God is not to complain about his hurt, nor, at the most fundamental level, even to seek relief from his pain. No, he should bow his knees in prayer, as he comes boldly and with confidence, to thank God that he is permitted to suffer in serving Christ. It is glorious to serve Him, even when it does occasion hardship, if only he will see it. Your task is to

15   from Whom the whole family in the heavens and on the earth is named,
16   that in keeping with His glorious riches, by His Spirit, He may make it possible for you to be strengthened with power in the inner person,
17   and that Christ will dwell in your hearts by faith. By becoming rooted and grounded in love
18   may you, together with all of the saints, have the capacity to get a grasp of how broad, how long, how high and how deep Christ's love is,

---

move him from a complaining, discouraged, griping person to one who appreciates the will of God as it is being worked out in his life.

The heavenly Father is the archetypal father (lit., the phrase reads, **"The Father of Whom every fatherhood is named"**). So, when psychologists tell us that a child who has not seen a good example of fatherhood in growing up will not only suffer from the lack of the model, but will find it difficult (if not impossible) to trust in God as a Father, they have it backwards. We must not to look to human fathering as the means of trusting our heavenly Father; indeed, we are to look to God in order to know what fathering ought to be like. Regardless of the kind of fathering with which one grows up (It couldn't have been all that good in the pagan backgrounds of these Christians), he could become a good father by learning about fatherhood from the Father of all fathers (v. 15).

Though there have been a number of digressions, Paul is still outlining his prayer for the churches to whom he writes. He is drawing near to the end. He wants the Father, rich in the wealth, and in all He does, by the Spirit **to strengthen them with power in the inner person**. That, of course, does not mean physical, but moral strength. The Spirit encourages, gives boldness (Acts 4), fortifies and energizes with the promises of His Word (cf. Luke 11:13). And, he wants Christ to dwell in this strengthening way in their hearts ("heart" is the same as **"inner person"**) by faith.

How? By **becoming rooted and grounded in love** (v. 17b). When one becomes firmly established (rooted and grounded) in love, he knows what love is, how to express it, when and where. In others words, he yearns and learns how to love God and his neighbor. Again, it is not that one has to have experienced love from another human being in order to know how to love, as some wrongly teach, but Christ's love is the model for all Christian love. That is why, as Paul expresses it, you must help your counselee to get a grasp of the various dimensions of His love (vv. 18,19). In teaching love, describe God's love in Christ to your counselee. That is his Standard. Why would you use a lesser one? In learning **some-**

19 and to know something of His love which surpasses knowledge, so that you may be filled with all God's fullness.

20 Now to Him Who is able to do infinitely more than all that we ask or think, in keeping with the power that is working in us,

21 to him be glory in the church and in Christ Jesus to all generations forever and ever. Amen.

---

thing of the love of God in Christ—a love we never will be capable of fully understanding—your counselee will learn how to become filled with fullness of love from God Himself. What it takes to fill us to capacity is less than the love He exhibited toward us that, indeed, passes all knowledge. But, above all, do not forget that the model by which one may come to know what love is like, is the love of God shown to poor sinners in Christ. And, that means, in the cross.

Now, Paul writes the great, encouraging benediction that we all appreciate so much (vv. 20, 21). The power of the Holy Spirit is boundless. Because of that God is able to do far more for us than we ever ask for or imagine. With a resource like that, how is it that the counselee with which you are working is telling you "I can't?" Your response? Something like this: "Of course you can't, by your own wisdom and strength, but by the infinite power of the Holy Spirit who dwells within, most assuredly you can." Turn to this verse, read it, and ask if he believes it. In the end, all counseling is simply a matter of faith (v. 17). The problem is not with God; He has provided more than one needs to love Him and his neighbor. The problem is that we don't avail ourselves of His mighty resources because we don't really believe that they exist and are there for our use. Bring your counselee face to face with this great promise and call on him to believe and act accordingly. Strengthened faith in God's promises inevitably leads to action.

The Holy Spirit is at work in every believer bringing about those things that please God, the works that God has prepared beforehand (cf. 2:10). To God belongs all the glory from the Church to our generation, and to all those that follow.

CHAPTER 4

1 So then, as a prisoner for the Lord, I urge you to walk in a way that is appropriate to the calling to which you were called,

---

Verse one of Chapter Four is the hinge on which the doctrinal chapters and the more practical ones swing. Although the preponderance of material in each of the two sections corresponds to these designations, we have already seen that doctrinal material can be practical. It is just as true that practical material presupposes doctrine.

Paul mentions his imprisonment; he is **a prisoner of the Lord**. It is the Lord that put him there, not the Jews or the Romans. How important for counselees to recognize this same truth; when they find themselves boxed up in some problem, they should first think, "The Lord has put me here. He must have a purpose for me in this situation; I shall find out what it is." By thinking this way, one immediately turns the focus away from self and from others, and what they may or may not have done, to the Lord, the One Whose will in the circumstance ought to be first and above all. From that perspective on the problem, it will look quite different. That is not to say that self or others, and their actions, should be ignored. Both must be held responsible for them. Rather, it should mean that what they have done should be viewed as serving God's larger purposes. From a realization of this, and an endeavor to get in line with what God is doing through the problem, the counselee can actually be brought to the place where he senses something of an adventure in the difficulty.

Note, throughout this book, I have been trying to bring the counselee to a place where he sees that his dealings are, at bottom, with the Lord and not with anyone else. All others, even those who may have wronged him, are but catalysts to this end. Counselors who counsel in that manner will discover that this makes all the difference in the world. And, remember, this is not some sort of impractical super-spiritual hogwash. It is the way Paul introduces the practical section of the letter. This mode of thinking is the most practical of all in that it undergirds everything and creates an atmosphere and groundwork for all else that you do.

If Paul, as a prisoner, with the humiliation, deprivation, hardship and suffering that imprisonment entails, could **walk in a way that is appropriate to God's calling**, so could those to whom he is writing. There is something of that note in his reference to his condition. But what is this

2   with complete humility and meekness, with patience putting up with
one another in love,

---

biblical term "**walk**"? The word, used throughout the Old and the New
Testaments, means "life-style." It is closely related to our "conduct." How
one *conducts* himself and how he *walks* are concepts practically synony-
mous in usage. So, in this latter half of the Book, Paul strikes the note of
the Christian's walk from the outset. Indeed, to do so is quite appropriate.
It is a theme carried out though Chapters 4,5,6. The word itself appears
here, in 4:17, 5:2, 5:8 and 5:15. But, even where it does not occur, the
theme of the believer's walk predominates.

This walk is not a *solitary* walk. Nor is it a walk with the Lord. It is
that, but more: it is a walk *with other Christians* that Paul has in view. He
is concerned to promote unity in the Church at all levels. He will discuss
how Christians should walk as husband and wife, child and parent and
owner and employee. And prior to, and basic to that walk he will set forth
the conditions for it in Chapter four: how one *talks* has a lot to do with
how one *walks*. Communication and the put off/put on dynamic are
uppermost among those things that make the Christian walk possible.
Naturally, these are the very things with which the Christian counselor
must busy himself day after day. Therefore, in his work of counseling, he
will find chapter four of the utmost value.

The walk should be **appropriate to the calling with which you
were called**. That is the bottom line. The calling was in grace. Your counselee must walk as one who received what he has by grace. Grace is God's
goodness freely given with no human merit in sight. All pride and boasting are excluded. One may exult in the Lord alone. One, therefore, is
called to love and serve the God who saved him.

This calling, as Paul goes on to say, should issue in **complete humility and meekness, with patience putting up with one another in love**.
Clearly, the Christian walk, here in view, is a walk (as I said) with other
Christians. Humility, meekness and patience are elements in the relationship of one believer with another. While each has an interior aspect, it is
the exterior aspect (which is the result of the interior) that is in view in
verse two. It is the way that these qualities affect the relationship between
believers that concerns Paul. Every one of these aspects of the walk is of
importance to counseling. For instance, take **humility**. **Humility** is the
opposite of arrogance and pride. What Paul is promoting is the opposite of
the modern self-esteem movement. To the Greek, as to many today,

3   doing your best to keep the unity of the Spirit by the bond of peace.
4   There is one body and one Spirit, just as when you were called there is one hope to which you were called.
5   There is one Lord, one faith, one baptism,
6   one God and Father of all, Who is over all and through all, and in all.

   7 Now grace was given to each one of us according to the measure that Christ determined.

---

humility was a vice. It meant weakness; it was opposed to self-respect. It was Christianity that brought to the world a different view of humility. But, in the world around, the original Pagan significance of humility is seeping back into our culture—even into the culture (if it can be called such) of the Church!

If a counselee exhibits behavior or speaks in language that conflicts with humility, biblically speaking, he needs to be confronted with the fact. He may be so heavily brainwashed by current teachings that he thinks of pride as a virtue, not a vice. Certainly that is the attitude inculcated even in our Christian schools when, if the football team happens to win the championship, all the fingers go up in unison, proudly indicating "We're no 1!" But progress cannot be made in living the Christian life unless humility is present. Humility comes from recognizing that all one has is of grace. Pride and arrogance come from considering one's achievements the result of his own strength and power. Humility is the result of recognizing that even one's next breath comes from God.

Meekness is the opposite of an attitude of criticism and faultfinding. It is not weakness. There is strength in it that stems from the ability to appreciate the good that God has done in another and in treating him with the gentleness that comes from knowing that God also is patient with him. It is the opposite of the attitude that says to another, "Well, I see you're in trouble. I could have told you so."

Love that enables the counselee to **put up with** another is essential to the Christian walk. Love is the quality that makes the other elements mentioned here possible. Only true love, *the willingness to give*, of one's time, concern, money or whatever it is that another needs, is becoming capable of putting up with those annoyances and outright insults and offenses that often come from other Christians. Apart from an attitude of giving, there will be no patience with another. Every one of these aspects of the Christian walk is important to counselees. Verse 2 contains a number of very sharp arrows for the counselor's quiver.

Why are these characteristics so vital? Because they are what con-

8   That is why it says, **Having ascended to the heights, He led His captives into captivity and gave gifts to the people.**
9   (Now, "Having ascended"—what meaning does this have unless He also had descended into the lower parts of the earth?
10   He Who descended is the same One Who also ascended far above all the heavens, that He might fill all things.)

---

tribute to **unity** among Christians (cf. v. 3). By creating the right sort of peace (not peace at any cost, but peace at a cost to one's self) they preserve **the unity of the Spirit**. The unity that already exists must be preserved, but that isn't enough: that unity must continually grow. The Spirit promotes peace and is grieved by turmoil in Christ's church. And here, through these words of Paul, inspired by Him, the Spirit tells us how to bring about and keep peace among believers.

Now, Paul describes that unity which is the result of the proper walk of Christians with one another (vv. 4-6). He wants the reader to think about seven unities that are uppermost in Christ's Church: **one body** (the invisible church), **one Spirit**, **one expectation** (the meaning of the word "hope" in Scripture) eternal life with Christ, **one Lord** (Jesus), **one faith** (deposited once for all with the apostles, and now for us in the Bible), **one baptism** (of the Spirit by which one is admitted into membership in the invisible body of Christ) and **one God and Father of all** [believers]. He is **over** all things, at work **through** all things and affecting His will **in** all things. Because this is so, believers ought to exhibit this unity.

However, biblical unity is not artificial, like the unity of a pile of stones, simply thrown together, but a unity like that of stones cemented together according to a master-builder's design. It is unity that results from acceptance, teaching and submission to the doctrinal truths that have just been listed in verses 4-6. Christians must become unified over, around and in truth. There is no cry for a shallow ecumenicalism here; what Paul has in mind (as he says plainly later on in the chapter) is a harmony of faith and life.

One of the things that often creates differences among believers is the disproportionate amount of **grace measured out by God**. Not everyone has the same amount. It was Christ Who determined who would have what. The unity of which he speaks, therefore, is a **unity in diversity**. More advanced Christians often become perturbed with less advanced ones, while the latter often look at the former with disdain. "Why can't he learn faster?" one asks, while the other says, "Who does he think he is to

> 11   He gave some as apostles, some as prophets, some as evangelists and
> some as shepherds and teachers,
> 12   to equip the saints for a work of service leading to the building up of
> Christ's body

push others so fast?" There must be a willingness not to put up either with sloth or undue pressure, but to freely accept true differences accruing from the varying measures of grace apportioned to each. How important this principle—that Christ Himself apportions grace in differing **measures**—is to a counselor when confronting either of these attitudes!

These proportions of grace are thought of as gifts out of the spoils of battle that a conquering general gives to the soldiers who fought for him. Jesus, the conquering Hero, **gave gifts** to His followers though the Spirit He sent when He **ascended** to the Father's throne on high. He is the One who came down to earth to become a man, and, as the God-man, ascended to the Father's throne. There, He **fills** the universe with His rule.

The gifts that He gave to His Church are also thought of as the officers in the Church (vv. 11-16). He **gave some as apostles, some as prophets, some as evangelists and some as shepherds and teachers**. As may be clearly seen in the original (the English is deceptive), there are four groups here: **apostles, prophets, evangelists, and pastor-teachers**. The last group is expressed by two characterizations (the two works of the elder: teaching and ruling).

Two of these offices are extinct (**apostles and prophets**). As we have already noted, they were foundational offices, through which revelation was given. The foundation has been laid, the revelation is in the Bible; there is no more need for either. **Evangelists** are what we now call missionaries—those who go to places where the gospel has not been heard to proclaim Christ and found churches. The **shepherd/teachers**, on the other hand, minister to the Church. They shepherd the flock and they teach the Word of God to them. Why? Verse 12 tells us: **to equip the saints for a work of service leading to the building up of Christ's body**. Note well that it is the *saints* who are to build up the body. The task of the shepherd/teacher is to equip them so that they will be able to carry on this work. Those two tasks (shepherding and teaching) are also the two tasks of the counselor. This is natural since God planned for Christian counseling to be a function of His church in equipping saints who need such help.

No counselor can rightly shirk the responsibility to **teach**. Yet, some

13   until we all attain to the unity of the faith and to the full knowledge of God's Son, to mature manhood, to the point where we become as fully adult as Christ.

14   This must happen so that we may no longer be infants, blown about and carried around by every wind of teaching, by human trickery, by craftiness designed to lead to error.

---

counselors do not like to teach. Others seem to think that to teach God's truth to someone who may be especially susceptible in a time of need is unethical. It is not. It is never wrong to teach God's truth *in the right way.* That means that there is no trickery, that there is a clear presentation of what one has to say and that it is accompanied with the caution that God does not countenance "foxhole conversions." After all, God may have brought this counselee to the end of his rope in order to lead him to faith. When people see that they do not have the answers to life's questions, it is not wrong to ask them, "Well, don't you think it is now about time to listen to God's answers?"

Shepherding, of course, means caring for the sheep. Counselors often welcome this side of the task. But, it means more than giving sage advice. Shepherding means seeing to it that the counselee becomes an integral part of a flock under a shepherd. That, too, is part of the counseling task that is neglected by too many counselors.

And the goal of this teaching and shepherding is set forth in verse 13 where Paul says the same thing four different ways:

   1. to attain unity of the faith;

   2   to gain a full knowledge of Christ;

   3. to grow to mature manhood;

   4. to become as fully adult as Jesus.

This edificational work, brought about by shepherding and teaching from God's Word, **must happen**, says Paul, so that becoming mature, Christians **may no longer be able to be blown about by every wind of teaching, human trickery and craftiness that leads to error**. God is concerned about truth and its place in establishing one so that he may not be easily moved from the truth. That is why it is not enough for counselors to deal with superficial matters, or the so-called practical issues, apart from doctrine. Doctrine is what establishes, matures, and thus, enables one to walk the Christian life securely.

So, it is the task of the counselor to be constantly **speaking the truth in love**. It is truth, you see, that establishes and, like food, helps one **to**

15 But by speaking the truth in love we may grow up in all respects into Him Who is the Head, that is, Christ,
16 from Whom the whole body fitted together and harmoniously joined together by every joint that is provided, in keeping with the proportion of effort contributed by each individual part, brings about the growth of the body so as to build itself up by love.

---

grow up in all respects into Him Who is the Head of His Church, even Christ. There is, then, for counselors who wish to see their counselees grow into mature Christians, no way to avoid the task of teaching truth. That does not mean that you are going to cram it down people's throats. Truth must be taught **in love**. As we saw, love is *giving,* the very opposite of *getting.* One gives himself to the communication of truth. He is patient, meek, humble and kind in his teaching. He is like His Lord Who, in an invitation to learn from Him, described Himself as **meek and humble in heart** (Matthew 11:28-30). In that powerful picture of Christ as the teacher Who is easily approached, we see also that it is He from Whom one may find refreshment in His teachings. There you have the description of the ideal teacher. If you want to learn how to teach, explore His words in those three verses.

What is the object of the teaching? The **maturity** of faith that enables your counselee to become more like Christ (v. 15), Who is **the Head** of His Church.

This Lord of the Church, so works through every part that the entire body **builds itself up by love** (v. 16). In this verse Paul uses the physiological terms of the Greek medical writers. The words may pertain to the system of nerves and muscles. But, be that as it may, in His plan, **each part of the body contributes something to the growth** of the whole. That is how He intends the Church to grow (cf. I Corinthians 16:15ff). And the element that runs through all is **love**. The sum of the commandments, as well as the new commandment, is love. Therefore, counselor, your work is to promote godly love. Anything you do that diminishes love must be removed from your counseling practice; everything biblical that promotes it must be incorporated into it. Why not take the time, at some point, to examine every principle and practice you follow, to see if it truly does promote love? Does ventilation? Does promoting self-esteem? Does a twelve-step approach? Think about this carefully.

We now turn to the second half of the chapter. A section that is a very important part of the biblical counselor's arsenal. We shall take the time to

17   So then, I say and testify this together with the Lord, that you must no longer walk like the gentiles do in their meaningless ways of thinking—
18   their understanding is darkened, and they are total strangers to God's life because of the ignorance that is in them resulting from the hardness of their hearts.
19   They have lost all sensitivity and have given themselves to sensuality, greedily becoming involved in every sort of uncleanness.

---

work our way through it with care (especially beginning with verse 21). First, let's consider verses 17-20.

In these four verses, Paul describes the condition of the unsaved Gentile. His **thinking is meaningless, his understanding is darkened, he is a total stranger to God's way of life, his heart is hardened (lit., "thickened") against the truth, he has lost all sensitivity because he has given himself to sensuality, and, greedily, he has given himself over to every sort of uncleanness.** What a remarkable description of the sort of things that we see in contemporary society—with the approval of leaders of all sorts! These sins of which they approve at length bring people to counseling. So counselors should take heed to the description. The loss of **sensitivity** by sensualists, for instance, is an insight into sexual promiscuity that every counselor should have (v. 19). Having become sated with it, one ceases to enjoy or appreciate it after a while. The **darkened understanding, ignorance and meaningless ways of thinking** account for the foolish decisions made by the public and by many governing officials. One wonders where the stupidity will end! But, apart from the Standard of truth and sensibility found in God's Word, men can do little more than flounder.

Well, Paul doesn't outline these problems aimlessly. He wants every Christian to free himself from them. That is the purpose of his sweeping command in verse 17: **you must no longer walk as the Gentiles do.** In one stroke of the brush, that contrasts the Christian's walk that is appropriate to his calling in Christ with that of the unsaved multitude, he makes it clear that there must be a brand new walk, or life-style. Counselors must take heed. It is not just this problem or that you must grapple with, but the problem of *a life-style* that God wants changed. And, he introduces verse 17 with the emphatic words, **I say and testify this together with the Lord.** Those expressions are parallel to our "now hear this," or "If you get anything at all be sure to get this."

Now, if every convert were counseled immediately about the various aspects of his life-style and told that, "obviously, your business policies,

20 You, however, didn't learn that sort of thing from Christ
21 (if indeed you heard Him and were taught by Him according to the truth that is in Jesus)!

---

your home life, your social contacts, etc., all must be reviewed and we must start you on a new course of life in *every* area, there would be less counseling to do later on. When one first comes to Christ, he is malleable, having that "first love" to motivate him, so that it would be much easier to begin counseling then, across the board. Later, when the old life-style that he brings into his Christian experience has hardened, it is far more difficult. All he wants in counseling is to solve some problem that bothers him. Usually, if you will investigate, even a little bit, you will see that underneath that "problem" lies a much bigger one—the need for a radical change of life-style. This change begins with a revitalization of thinking and ends with a vast improvement in living. Notice, as Paul describes the situation, how the **thinking** of the Gentile leads to his **living**.

Having described the unsaved life of the Gentiles, Paul says **You, however, didn't learn that sort of thing from Christ.** Christ instructs His children in the way to life by His servants who preach and counsel them according to His Word. Those who are true to it, receive the very message of Christ Himself, so that it can be said that they learned it "from Christ." That is how important the communication of the truth of Scripture is. Counselors and preachers must never downplay the critical nature of what they are doing. Either they are teaching what Christ wants taught in such a way that *their teaching can be said to be His*, or they are not. That is a fearful responsibility; one either properly represents the Lord in what he teaches or he *misrepresents* Him. That is why counselors must become adept in their understanding and use of the Bible. There is no place for the counselor who does not spend hours devouring the Scriptures, studying in-depth what God has to say. His is a trust that is given, a stewardship, as Paul called it, in which he must prove faithful.

In verse 21, he asks them to consider the possibility that they may not have **heard and believed** Christ's truth, but something else purporting to be it. That danger always exists, and when counselees fail to make progress, after investigating all other possibilities, one may want to ask this question in counseling: "Have you truly heard and believed the gospel of Christ?"

Notice the emphasis on **learning** (v. 20) and **teaching** (vv. 21,22). That is what we are principally concerned with at the outset. False teach-

22   You were taught regarding your previous habit patterns to put off the
old person that you were, who is corrupted by deceitful desires,
23   being rejuvenated in the attitude of your mind,

---

ing or the failure to teach, on the one side, and the lack of learning on the
other, are often matters to investigate. Many Christians are brought into
the Christian faith with little or no instruction and with no idea whatso-
ever that there must be radical changes in their walk (that is, across the
board in every area of their lives). Jesus is presented as a kind of add-on,
who can make your present life more pleasant and who will eventually
take you to heaven. They have no concept of the dramatic differences that
Jesus wants to make in them. Counselors, when they encounter this phe-
nomenon, like Paul, must question what they have been taught. They may
have a task on their hands, informing them for the first time what it means
to have Christ in one's life.

Now, for the concluding material, information that is so vital to the
counselor that he could not do without it. Verse 22 reads, **You were
taught regarding your previous habit patterns.** The difficulty is that
virtually no one *is* taught today regarding the habits that he acquired
before becoming a Christian and what to do about them. That is one of the
principal reasons why counselors have so much work to do. That Gentile
life-style is a matter of sinful patterns that the corrupt nature with which
you were born has habituated into your thinking and your behavior.
Because you bring these patterns into the new life when you are converted, you need to be taught what to do about them. But virtually no
Christians are.

Habit is very much a part of your life. If you were to remove all habits, you couldn't get along. The capacity to do things by habit—i.e., automatically, unconsciously, skillfully and comfortably (the four characteristics of a habit)—is a blessing of God. It is what enables you to do two
things at once. You can drive and talk. You can instantly put the brakes on
when the car before you flashes its brake lights. You can eat while listening to the radio. Indeed, habit is so much a part of your moment-by-
moment living that you don't realize it. Doing things by habit, we say, is
"second nature." You do them as if you were born with them.

But, in a world of sin, every blessing may be turned into a curse. Sinners learn from the earliest days to program into the habit capacity all
sorts of sinful responses, which, in turn, become a part of them. When hit,
they hit back—harder. When someone says something uncomplimentary

24 and to put on the new person that you are, who is created in God's
likeness with righteousness and holiness that come from the truth,

---

about them, they retort with something equally so. And so it goes. It is
these sinful habit patterns that make up the Gentile life-style according to
which Paul says, **You can walk no longer.** The teaching, then, that the
counselor must do is the teaching that should have been done as soon as
the new convert professed faith in Christ. Much of what he does is belated
work that should have been done by the evangelist.

This teaching is **according to the truth that is in Jesus** (v. 22[b]). In
other words, the Bible has what is needed to do the job. There is no need
for extra-scriptural teaching. This teaching consists of one fundamental
dynamic: the put off/put on dynamic found in vv. 22, 24. The old person,
that one was, prior to conversion, like a discarded garment, must be put
off. The "old person" is the old you with your sinful life-style. It is
important to get rid of the old patterns, to become dehabituated. But, let
us ask, when is a liar not a liar? When is a thief not a thief? When he stops
lying? Wrong; he is still a liar, who happens at the moment not to be
lying. When he stops stealing? Wrong. He is simply a thief between jobs!

Well, then, when is a liar no longer a liar; a thief no longer a thief?
When he has put on the biblical alternative—that is, when it has become
habituated into his walk. It is not enough to put off the old ways; if they
are not replaced with biblical ways, one will revert to them. One cannot
simply *break* a habit; he must *replace* it. That is the teaching that is necessary for a counselor to engage in: teaching counselees how to replace sinful habit patterns with their biblical alternatives.

The **old person** (the you wrongly habituated) is **corrupted** by following **deceitful desires**. They are deceitful because they promise what
they cannot deliver—peace and joy. He leads a feeling-oriented life-style.
In this life-style, decisions are made on the basis of desire-fulfillment.
That must change. He must learn instead to do those things that are oriented toward true righteousness and holiness; he must learn a command-
ment-oriented life-style. Decisions are made on the basis of whether one's
thoughts, words, actions and attitudes please God. And this, in turn, is
determined by the commands and principles laid out in the Bible

So, true change that is pleasing to God, is a two-factored process:
one must not only remove the former habituated patterns, but must likewise replace them with their biblical alternatives. Every counselor must
learn how to help counselees to do this. It is absolutely crucial to counsel-

25 So then, putting off lying, **each one must speak truth with his neighbor**, since we are members of one another.

---

ing to be able to do so.

But what is the motivating force necessary to bring this off? Verse 23 tells us. The counselee **must be rejuvenated in the attitude of his mind**. The word for "renewed" that Paul uses here is not the same as the one used in Romans 12, or in the parallel passage in Colossians. In those two places, the verb simply says "renew." It gives no hint about *how* this renewal may take place. Here, the word used means, "to make youthful again." That is "to rejuvenate." It is easy to become cynical. But one must come to the place where he sees that it is worthwhile to make these changes **for Christ's sake**. If he does not have pleasing Him at the bottom of all that he does, he will not make the effort. The anticipation of youth, with all its possibilities, must be renewed, replacing the cynicism that corrodes throughout life. When he recognizes that it is worth while serving Christ, he will be motivated to change—and not before.

Well, when is a liar not a liar? Verse 25 makes that clear. When he has so changed his life-style that, having put off lying, in those circumstances where he lied before, he now automatically, unconsciously, skillfully and comfortably tells the truth. It is one thing not to lie; another to tell the truth. One may learn to avoid a direct answer, and not lie ("How do you like my new dress?" "Oh, isn't it nice to have a new dress!"). But it is more difficult to tell the truth when God requires it.

Well, how about the thief: when is a thief no longer a thief? Verse 28 makes that clear. When he has been rehabituated so that he *gives* to those truly in need out of the earnings of his own hands. Until then, one can protest all he wants about having changed; I'll believe him when I see this new life-style in place.

The liar disturbs any body of which he is a part—a church, a school, a home. He is a member of that body, says Paul (25[b]), and as such needs to communicate truth to the other members of the body. Otherwise, everything goes haywire. Tell the teenage boy who clams up this, or the wife who refuses to talk about problems or about her thoughts. If people don't have the truth, they will make bad decisions, contrary to the best interests of the body. It is like the knees having the information that they should bend so that the body may sit in a chair and the hand thinking it is time to remove the chair. It is because of such communication failure that Christians are always pulling the chair out from beneath one another. A good

26 **Be angry, but don't sin**; don't let the sun set on your angry mood.

27 Don't give the devil a toehold.

28 The thief must stop stealing; instead he must labor, working with his own hands at honest work, so that he may have something to share with those who have need.

29 Don't let a single rotten word come from your mouths, but rather, whatever is good for constructively meeting problems that arise, so that your words may help those who hear.

---

counselor is prepared always to stress the importance of truthful communication as the way to smooth functioning among the members of any body. And, he will work according to the put off/put on dynamic to achieve that communication.

In verse 26, the way to deal with **anger** is set forth. Usually the anger displayed by counselees is improper, being aroused by words or actions from others that should never occasion anger at all, or by the wrong sorts of attitudes in the counselee himself. There are, however, times when anger is certainly justified—as this verse indicates. One may **be angry but not sin**. How is that? Well, first of all, he does not blow up (v. 31 disposes of that as an option). On the other hand, he may not clam up (v. 31 also eliminates that option, because clamming up leads to bitterness). Rather, he must follow the biblical middle between these two erroneous extremes: he must deal with the problem right away. He may **not allow the sun to go down on his anger**. Some counselees, you will discover, have let many moons go down!

Rather, he must do as Paul directs in verse 29. There, he says that one must not let any **rotten word** (lit., putrid word) **pour out of the mouth**. That is not referring principally to what we call dirty talk. It is referring to talk that tears another down. But, on the contrary, his words are to build up the offender. They must be words that are aimed at **constructively solving the problem** rather than blowing up or becoming bitter and hardened. All the energy that might otherwise be released out of control (blowing up) or that may be held in (clamming up) is to be released, under control, in working toward a biblical solution to **the problem that has arisen**. And, it is to be done as quickly as possible: the sun is not to go down before at least the initial attempts to solve the problem have been put into motion.

When one refuses to do something quickly, the devil **gains a toehold** in the church and in the lives of those concerned. They are on their way toward division, something earnestly desired by the wicked one. By the

30 And don't grieve God's Holy Spirit with Whom you were sealed for the redemption day.

31 All bitterness and anger and wrath and clamor and blasphemy must be removed from you, along with every sort of evil,

32 and be kind to one another, tenderhearted, forgiving each other just as God in Christ forgave you.

---

way they counsel, some encourage waiting too long for change.

The only place where the Scriptures speak of **grieving the Holy Spirit** is in verse 30 in the midst of this discussion of the right sort of Christian communication. Not only does the devil rejoice when Christians fight, the Holy Spirit is grieved. These two facts may be mentioned with some force when you encounter counselees who are tearing the church or their marriages (or both) apart.

Summing up, Paul lists the things that must go—the Gentile patterns that must be replaced with biblical ones. They include **bitterness** (anger not dealt with properly causes this), and **anger** (occasioned wrongly; unrighteous anger), **wrath** (pouring out vindictive words or doing vindictive acts) and **clamor** (causing scenes in front of others that disturb the peace) and **blasphemy** (not only against God but against anyone—it means hard words spoken against someone), and **every sort of evil** (the catch-all that keeps a counselee from thinking if he does other things that are evil, he is OK, because they are not mentioned specifically in this list).

If all of those things are to be removed from the Christian and no longer remain as a part of his life-style, then what must replace them? Some things are mentioned in verse 31: **kindness, tenderheartedness, forgiving attitudes**. Where these are present, it is rare that anything of the sort mentioned in verse 30 will occur. Our forgiveness is to be modeled on the forgiveness we have received in Christ (For details on forgiveness, see my book, *From Forgiven to Forgiving*.). And, this last statement is deftly inserted at the conclusion of the discussion in order to motivate as well.

The chapter is powerful, it sets forth the goals and methods for attaining them, that, in one way or another, nearly every counseling session involves. Become familiar with them and use them to the full.

The first two verses of Chapter Five actually form the conclusion to the entire argument and should have been made a part of Chapter Four. Forgive as **God, in Christ forgave you**. So, then, he says, **be imitators of God, as dear children** who imitate their parents. Imitation is a powerful learning method. And, not only in forgiveness, but in every sort of way, one must learn to imitate God. Fathers, imitate God's fatherly discipline, love, care. Elders, imitate the shepherding care of God over His people, etc. In any way possible to do so, counselees may be called upon to ask themselves "How does God treat others?" and follow His example.

The final word, then, is that this Christian walk is a walk in love; it is the same sort of life-style that Christ followed when He, out of love, gave up Himself for us, an offering of which God highly approved (it was fragrant to Him). There you have it. Paul provides help in moving from a meaningless way of living to the life of Christ in loving sacrifice. That is the change God desires in everyone who professes faith in Jesus.

CHAPTER 5

1 So then, be imitators of God, like dear children,

2   and walk in love, in the same way that Christ loved us and gave Himself up for us as a fragrant offering and sacrifice to God.

3 But there must not even be the slightest mention of sexual sin and of
any sort of uncleanness or greediness among you, as is proper for saints.

In the concluding portion of the comments made on Chapter Four, I
considered verses 1-2 of the present chapter since they form a conclusion
to what was said previously and, properly speaking, belong to the discussion contained there. Therefore, I shall begin with verse 3 of chapter 5.
Moving smoothly from what he had said about anger and poor communication because of lying, etc., to another disruptive element, Paul wrote,
But there must not even be the slightest mention of sexual sin... By
this, he is saying that one of the things that greatly displeases God is sexual license. That is true because it is a violation of His commandment, it is
the desecration of another person and it is a disruptive element in any congregation. Few things shake up congregations as much as the pastor running off with the Church secretary or organist. Or an elder or deacon
divorcing his wife after committing adultery with another member of the
Church. Or, even when two young people become sexually involved with
one another. All these sins have an extremely unsettling effect.

But what does Paul mean by **not even the slightest mention of sexual sin** or **any sort of uncleanness or greediness among you?** Does he
refer to our speech or to our actions? Well, some have taken this to mean
that Christians should never *talk* about sexual sin. But, if that were the
true interpretation of Paul's words, these very paragraphs—not to speak
of many other places in his writings—would be a violation of the prohibition. No, what he is saying is "Let me not even hear a whisper of that sort
of thing going on in your midst." And, again, by that he doesn't mean "If
it is occurring, cover it up; I don't want you to appear to be anything but
perfect." Rather, in a strong way, Paul is saying don't become involved in
sexual sin at all! To not **hear** even the **slightest mention** of such a thing
means that there must not be even the slightest suspicion that such sin is
occurring—because it is not.

Too often, when sexual sin does occur, people do try to cover it up.
Instead, here the apostle openly confronts that tendency. That he must do
so is indicative of the fact that sexual sin then, as well as now, was a real

4 There must not be obscene and stupid talk or dirty joking, none of which is appropriate to you; but instead there should be thanksgiving.

---

problem for Christians to overcome. Indeed, what he is doing here is to encourage them to face and conquer it. Counselors must do no less.

The phrase "any sort of uncleanness" refers, beyond adultery, to everything else condemned by the Scriptures as sexual sin. Doubtless all sorts of things bordering on and leading to the actual commission of such sin are also included. The phrase should interest counselors, because it seems to go beyond the commandments not to fornicate, or commit the act, to everything suggestive of it. That covers many issues often debated by counselees. Verse 4 explains: **There must be no obscene and stupid talk or dirty joking.** Those words seem epexegetical (explanatory) of the phrase "any sort of uncleanness." They do not include everything that is comprehended by the phrase, but go to the outer limits of that to which it refers, thereby indicating how far reaching the command is since it would include any and everything between joking about and committing the sin itself. Because there are many situations that counselees consider doubtful these verses may be used to clear up those doubts. It is important for counselors to know, to understand and be able to reproduce the argument above (in some communicable form) to those who think that they can play around the edges of sexual sin. Think long and hard about the import of Paul's words.

Because *greediness* for anything is like the lust many have for sexual expression, both of which are inappropriate for saints (vv. 3,4), Paul packages his thoughts into a double-barreled prohibition. *Neither* of these strong desires is right Can't you see the greedy person, like the sexual offender, smacking his lips at the very thought of sinful opportunities that lay ahead of him? At any rate, the greedy person, who may speak long and hard against fornication, may be powerfully shown the severity of his sin of greed (a thing not widely acknowledged today *as sin* in Church circles) by the fact that Paul lumps it together with sexual sins of every sort. And, in addition, he calls both the greedy and the sexual offenders idolaters (v. 5). It is possible for counselees to set up things or persons as objects for which they live—and ultimately *worship*. This is the most common form of idolatry into which Christians are liable to fall.

Of course, counselees will make every sort of excuse in the book for their covetousness. "After all," they will tell you, "I am only trying to provide for my family." But often, when you carefully examine how they are

5   You can by sure of this—that sexually immoral persons, or unclean persons or greedy persons (who are idolaters) don't have an inheritance in the empire of Christ and of God.

"caring" for the family, you will discover that it is true that the family actually suffers from the greed that is exhibited. When the family suffers from inordinate amounts of time spent in work, from two parent jobs that are unnecessary, from unnecessary purchases that decimate income, etc., you can point out those facts. "This," you may observe, "is not a matter of providing for your family, but, rather, of providing for the satisfaction of your own lusts (desires)."

Counselor, when was the last time you centered in on the counselee's *speech*? There is every reason to do so, whether it is sexually tainted or obviously the product of greed (v. 4). Don't let him dismiss your comments with the reply that he is "only talking." That is precisely Paul's point—he is talking **in an inappropriate way** about such things. As we saw, there is nothing wrong in talking about sex or greed properly (these very verses do); Paul refers to that talk which is improper; in particular, joking about such matters suggestively.

The put on, to replace the put off (just described), is speech filled with **thanksgiving**. One should be grateful for all God has done to free him from lewdness and greed. And, if he must talk, let him express such views. However, one must be careful at this point: it is easy to turn a testimony or a prayer—OR A COUNSELING SESSION— into a means of titillating others (including you). You must be very clear about such matters. You may find it essential to warn your counselee of such possibilities. If human beings find ways to turn prayer about other offences into gossip, surely they are capable of doing damage through prayer in sexual or greedy ways. That means that the thanksgiving must not only be genuine but must be carefully expressed. Even when one's intentions are honorable, if his expressions of thanksgiving are not carefully thought through and appropriately worded, they can still be offensive. Paul wants every Christian to be extremely careful about what he does in these matters. Words are important. Otherwise he would not make the effort to express these thoughts from so many different angles. You must study words and their effect. And, you must become a wordsmith, properly expressing *your* thoughts in counseling.

Then comes the warning—verse 5. People whose life-styles are *characterized* by greed and by sexual sin are not Christians. If one's life is

6   Don't let anyone swindle you by empty words; it is because of these things that God's wrath is going to come upon the sons of disobedience.
7   Therefore, don't participate with them in these things.

---

so dominated by a sin that he can be described by it above all other descriptions of his life-style (a gossip, rather than a housewife, for instance), he is clearly unsaved. True, Christians can offend by committing all the same sins; that's obvious from the exhortations in the previous verses. But those who refuse to obey, and who make no progress in overcoming such difficulties, should take heed to the warning—and counselors, in those cases, should not be hesitant to issue it.

The warning continues in verse 6 from a different perspective—be careful not to listen to anyone who would **swindle you with empty words**. There are those who seem to say that if you have ever walked the aisles of a church or made a profession of faith you certainly are saved, no matter how you live. It is against any such teaching that verse 6 is directed. God hates sin and will pour out his wrath from heaven on sinners who do nothing to forsake it. A profession of faith must be *genuine*. That means it must be more than words. If there is no obedience to His commands (we are not talking about perfection), no perceptible change, then why should we believe that the profession was genuine? After all, saving faith leads to works (as we have seen in Chapter two). The **sons of disobedience** are those who, "like father, like son," continue to engage in the acts of their father the devil. Counselors must be willing to encounter this problem and not gloss over it. The fact that one makes no progress at all may indicate that he is not a subject for counseling, but for evangelism. Counseling may lead to putting such persons out of the church if they do not come to faith in Christ.

And, according to verse 7, it is often because Christians associate with unbelievers of this stamp that they become like them. They soon find themselves "participating" in the same sins as unbelievers. That, too, is one reason why counselors often find it difficult to disengage their counselees from sinful sexual activity and greed—friends and associates of counselees may strongly encourage it all week long.

Often, breaking up bad associations is the key to helping the counselee. Obviously, if he is too weak to become the positive influence, he is being influenced negatively. In every association, one is either influencing or being influenced. It is often important to help the counselee to determine which, in his case, is true. See the discussion of this matter on I Cor-

8   At one time you were darkness, but now you are light in the Lord; walk as children of light
9   (the fruit of the light is seen in all sorts of goodness and righteousness and truth),
10   determining by testing what is pleasing to the Lord.
11   Don't take part in the unfruitful works of darkness; but instead even go so far as to expose them

---

inthians 15:33. Unless you take this matter seriously, everything you build up in counseling sessions will be torn down during intervening days.

Verses 8-14 turn on the truth that Christians have been enlightened by Christ. If so, why continue to have anything to do with the unfruitful works of darkness?—that is Paul's point. Instead, your counselees' goal should be to **walk as children of light**. Here the word for **children** differs from the word **sons** in verse 6. In verse 6, the formal, legal term is used. In verse 8, it is the tender, warm term for a loved family member. When one has come to faith in Christ, it is like the sunrise coming into his life. No longer does he need to walk in darkness; he knows where he is headed and can see the way. He is not lost, searching; he is traveling toward a destination. And, at length, he will reach it. So, his **walk** (life-style) should be that of a person who is enlightened by God's truth found in God's Word.

If he has truly been enlightened by the gospel, it is a matter, then, of looking for the fruit that such enlightenment inevitably produces (v. 9). One who is truly in the light neither can nor wants to hide that fruit. As Paul says, it will be *seen* **in all sorts of goodness and righteousness and truth** (v. 9). These things please the Lord. But how does one know what pleases Him? Your counselee must **determine by testing** (v. 10). How is this done? Well, one tests in terms of the fruit mentioned in verse 9. If the fruit of one's activity is in accord with the Scriptures, it is pleasing to the Lord. The Bible is the only Standard by which to determine what is good, righteous and true. You may have to spend time teaching counselees how to determine from the Bible what is pleasing to the Lord. My book, *What to do on Thursday,* may prove of help in showing you how to do so.

All the **unfruitful works of darkness** (that are an essential part of the unsaved **walk**) must be laid aside and the counselee must go even one step farther: he must **expose them**. To expose sin in others is a tricky business. Counselors must help counselees to thread their way safely through the minefields here. It is easy for a Christian to develop a superior attitude toward "those unsaved sinners!" Any such thing surely displeases God.

12   (it is disgraceful even to speak about the things that they do in secret).

He is no better than the one who is committing the sin that is exposed. He is saved by grace alone. Never let him forget that fact. In exposing sin in others, therefore, the Christian should be warned about his motives. Is he trying to show how much better he is or is he rightly concerned for the salvation of one committing sin, and for God, Who is dishonored by it? These sorts of questions must be considered whenever urging counselees to expose sin.

That means, also, that when you tell a repentant, adulterous counselee that it is important for the one with whom he committed adultery to tell her husband, you do so for the benefit of all concerned. When she insists she "can't" or "won't," the counselor must inform her that it is his duty to blow the whistle, since God has required him to seek forgiveness of her husband for his sin against him. But all of this should be done in such a manner that it *grieves* the counselee to have to expose sin. And, he will probably want the counselor to accompany him in doing so, in order to help pick up the pieces of this marriage. But, he first urges the wife to tell her husband, since it would be better for both if he hears first from her. If the counselor rightly steers matters along, that can be the beginning of the healing of relationships. He may be able to say to the husband, "You see, she is repentant and has taken the first step toward reestablishing proper relationships between the two of you."

But, as verse 12 indicates, the counselor must be careful not to become too personal about sexual sin. There are counselors who "get their kicks" out of wallowing in the details of a sexual liaison. That is sin; a type of voyarism. Every counselor must, therefore, be extremely careful to go only so far in eliciting and discussing matters of detail as is necessary. Anything that titillates him is wrong.

Things that go on under the cover of darkness (**in secret**) are disgraceful, and not to be talked about in detail. Sometimes those to whom you are exposing the sin want to do this ("How many times did you have sex with her, and what positions did you use?"). The counselor, turning to this passage, should curtail all such discussions. Often the one confessing the sin thinks he or she must "tell all" (in the same sense of going into all sorts of shameful details). Not so. This passage forbids it. You must be quick to discern when this sort of transgression of rightful boundaries is starting to take place and rapidly put a stop to it. As you can see, then, it is

13 Now everything that is exposed by the light is made visible; when everything is visible, there is light.

14 Therefore it says, "Wake up, you sleeper; arise from the dead and Christ will shine on you."

---

essential for the counselor to have his own life in shape when it comes to dealing with sexual matters. Be scrupulous about this. And, if ever dealing with a person of the opposite sex whose marriage partner is not present, you should make it a practice to be sure an elder *is* present with you.

Light exposes things. In darkness, it is hard to make out the landscape, but when it dawns, things take on their true shape. You see things as they are. Before you were saved, you were in darkness; now you are in light and you see sin for what it is (v. 13). Those who have acquired biblical light about false views of man, his problems and what to do about them, cannot help but expose the errors of non-biblical counseling. They should do so, however, not in a spirit of superiority, but in order to honor Christ and help His people. Even by the way the counselor discusses problems, when making no attempt to do so, his words will expose error and sin in counseling. He cannot do otherwise; light, by its very nature, exposes **everything**.

And, in order to reinforce the point, Paul quotes Isaiah 26: 19; 60:1. It is time to stop acting like you are still asleep in darkness. **Arise** out of the death sleep of the old life and go outside your house where the light of Christ can further illumine you (v. 14). There are times when you need to urge the very same thing.

Verses 15-20 form the next unit to consider. They are thoughts that have occurred to Paul during his previous discussions, but that he did not find the right place to insert. So, he bunches them up here at the end of the first half of the 5th chapter (which may be divided into two segments: vv. 1-20; vv. 21-33. Although, the latter should probably extend through 6:9).

Again, the theme of the believer's **walk** takes a prominent place (v. 15). The reader here is advised to **be careful** about how he walks. Many counselees have problems with this very thing: they are careless about their life-style. The solution to the problem lies in being wise, rather than unwise or foolish (vv. 15,17). Wisdom is a principal concern of the Bible. It is not the mere acquisition of knowledge, but, beyond that, the ability to use that knowledge in biblical ways that are appropriate to specific persons and situations. There is an entire genre of biblical literature called "wisdom literature." It is truth practically applied. At this point many

15 So then, see to it that you are careful about how you walk, not as unwise but as wise people,

16 taking advantage of the time because the days are evil.

17 Therefore, don't be foolish, but rather understand what the Lord's will is.

18 Don't get drunk with wine, since that leads to utter ruin, but rather be filled by the Spirit,

---

counselees stumble; they do not know how to apply truth. That is understandable, however, since all too few churches teach their members how to use the Bible in a practical way. They are more interested in having members recite rote facts. They rarely go beyond this to help them learn how to put wheels on those facts. The counselor must spend time, therefore, in becoming adept at showing and teaching such skills.

In the specific case in the passage, one is wise if he takes **advantage of the time**, knowing that **the days are evil**. Both counselors and counselees should heed this admonition. It is easy to waste valuable time in counseling. There is no way that this time can be redeemed. It is, therefore, important to make the most of each session, and to not allow counselees to waste time in sessions, coming back again and again without doing their weekly homework assignments. Just this week, I canceled a counseling session because the counselees failed to advance at all during the week, telling them that I would set the date for the next counseling session when they had achieved some results at the conference table that they were assigned to do. There are too many persons who enjoy the give and take of counseling without really wishing to make progress. And there are others who will not move until pressure is applied. Let it be known that you are not playing games; you are doing business for the Lord!

Once more, the admonition to avoid **foolishness** is sounded (v. 17) along with a command to learn to **understand God's will** (see comments on vv. 9,10). The Lord's will, obviously, is that which pleases Him.

Verse 18 is important to the counselor because of its very clear directives about drug and alcohol abuse. Not only does it forbid drunkenness as the result of alcoholic over indulgence (and drugs that stupefy would surely qualify as well), but it outlines the procedure by which a counselor may help the habitual offender to overcome his addiction. The Holy Spirit and wine are set over against one another as two possible controlling influences in life. It is possible for one or the other to dominate. While one must not become **drunken**, because that **leads to utter ruin** (lit., "unsalvagableness"), he is exhorted to **be filled with (or by) the Spirit**.

19 speaking to each other; in psalms and hymns and spiritual songs singing and making music in your hearts to the Lord,
20 always giving thanks for everything to God the Father in the Name of
our Lord Jesus Christ.

When one is dominated by wine, every area of his life is affected by
it. He gets drunk and his wife chews him out for this. So he runs off to his
buddies down at the bar for consolation and to drown his problems.
Because he does, he has a hangover at work in the morning and his boss
gets on him about his sloppy work. Feeling bad about this, he stops at the
bar on the way home to get more consolation, comes home drunk and...
You fill in the rest. It is a never-ending circle, where each thing he does
wrong leads to another so that his entire life is soon dominated by drink.
Even his "solutions" create new and worse problems. Each area of his life
is taken over by drink so that he cannot do otherwise.

What is God's solution? To examine and help the counselee to work
on *every area* of his life. It is not enough to deal with the bottle. The bottle
has affected the whole man *in all areas*, The Holy Spirit, instead, must
take control of each and every one of these areas—social life, physical
life, home life, work life, etc.—replacing the bottle in each. When his
whole life is filled (dominated) by the Spirit (as we say "the auditorium is
filled" when every seat is occupied) the bottle will have been replaced.
But not until then. That does not mean that the person has become perfect;
it does mean, however, that the Spirit has taken over in each area and is
chasing the bottle's influence out of it. The counselee changes his relationship with his wife, develops an interest in people at church rather than
at the bar, replaces work done with a hangover with solid labor, etc. He
has begun to honor God in every area of his life. Since the bottle has
affected all, the Spirit must gain control in all. Working on any lesser front
will fail.

Rather than the raucous behavior of the drunk, the believer ought to
be able to **speak** fruitfully to other Christians and to learn from them (v.
19[a]). And he should rejoice in **singing** praise to God, both outwardly and
in his **heart**.

And, his attitude should be an attitude of **continual thanksgiving** for
all that God has done for him (review Chapter One), as He exalts Christ
by praying in His mediatorial Name. When you hear your counselee singing and humming God's praises, you will know things have changed!

We come now to the last section (actually the beginning of a unit that

21   Submit yourselves to one another out of respect for Christ:

22   Wives, submit yourselves to your own husbands as to the Lord,

23   since a husband is the head of his wife as Christ also is the Head of the church; He Himself is the Savior of the body.

---

extends through 6:9). It has to do with the basic authority/submission relationships of the Christian in his social situations. Verse 21 is the general statement introducing the unit: **Submit yourselves to one another out of respect for Christ.** This admonition does not mean, as some have foolishly thought, that husbands ought to submit to wives, parents to children and masters to slaves. That would destroy the entire section, were it true; there would be no submission contexts. All authority would be done away with. No, it is simply a general statement introducing the fact that in the following verses (mentioned above) Paul will address three relationships in which submission must take place: wives, children and slaves are to submit to the authority that God has given to husbands, parents and masters.

In the remainder of the fifth chapter, Paul deals with the first of three authority/submission relationships. This, and those that follow, are relationships that constitute elements in the Christian **walk**. In order for these to be fruitful, it is necessary to bring into them all the principles of Chapters Four and Five examined previously. They are the ways in which proper relationships are promoted. Therefore, in developing these authority/submission relationships for counselees, it will be well to refer back to them to fill in ways and means.

Paul begins with the wives (v. 22); they must submit themselves to their own (not someone else's) husbands, as to the Lord. They do not submit in order to please their husbands, nor do they do so because their husbands order them to, **but as to the Lord**. That means that they do this for the Lord's sake. They are concerned about pleasing Him. They do it because He has commanded them to do so.

But **submission** must be understood. Many false ideas are floating about concerning it. Because of this, I usually take the time to give a brief, but rather complete, lecture to the counselees who are in need of understanding submission. I tell them that I recognize there is much misunderstanding about submission, and that I want to explain what the Scriptures have to say about this all-important matter.

First it may be well to set forth the elements involved. Basically, they are two: *obedience and respect.* The question of obedience is dealt with in

24 But as the church is subject to Christ, so also should wives be to their husbands in everything.
25 Husbands, love your wives just as Christ loved the church and gave Himself up for her

---

I Peter 3:1-6 while, here, Paul deals with respect (cf. v. 33). There are two sorts of authority that one may respect. One is *dunamis,* internal authority. The other, *exousia,* externally-conferred authority. A police officer may stop you for going through a traffic light. But you don't say to him, "Officer, before I receive that ticket, let me ask you a few questions. What kind of father are you? How do you treat your wife?" No, you accept his externally-conferred authority without asking any questions about his internally-earned authority. The husband's authority is **exousia, not dunamis** (although his **dunamis** ought always be growing to match the **exousia**. The wife salutes the uniform, even when she has difficulty saluting the man. This is true because she submits **as to the Lord**. Fundamentally, her submission is submission to Jesus Christ, just as your submission to the policeman is submission, not to him, but to the state; it is a recognition of the One from Whom all true authority stems. The husband's authority is really Christ's authority.

She is to submit **since the husband is the head of his wife as Christ also is the head of His church; He Himself is the Savior of the body.** That is an important point. At the outset of the discussion, Paul describes the sort of headship he has in mind. It is not tyrannical; not the headship of Hitler or Stalin. It is not arbitrary. Rather, it is to be a headship like that which Christ exercises over His Church. Obviously, this qualification is of the utmost significance. In Chapter One, verse 22, Paul says that God the Father subjected all things under Christ **for the sake of His Church**. The husband's headship, when faithfully reflecting the headship of Christ, is exercised always **for the sake of** his wife. That means that, like Christ, in every decision he makes, he has her blessing and benefit in mind. He truly brings her into all considerations; he often puts her first, before his own desires. Every woman who recognizes that headship means that her husband must treat her as Christ treats His church ought to jump in the air and click her heels at least twice before hitting the floor. Headship is designed to bless her! But that is not all. He must be so willing to put her first, that a husband must be willing, if need be, to *die* for his wife (as her savior— v. 23; cf. v. 25[b]). She, in turn, should be willing to *live* for him (not for herself). But, there are times when decisions must be made on which hus-

117

26 so that He might sanctify her, cleansing her by the washing of water with the Word,

27 that He might present to Himself the church gloriously arrayed, not having spot or wrinkle or any such thing, but rather that she might be holy and without blemish.

28 In the same way, husbands ought to love their wives as they love their own bodies. Whoever loves his wife loves himself.

29 Nobody ever hated his own flesh, but rather nourishes and cherishes it just as Christ does for the church—

---

band and wife disagree. In such instances, though she may not like it, she must subject herself to his decision as the church does to Christ (v. 24). There is, of course, one exception to the word **everything** found in that verse. Obviously, it means everything *legitimate*. If a husband orders his wife to do something that is clearly sin, she may not obey. God gave no one the authority to command anyone to sin. If he asks her to become a partner in wife-swapping, she must refuse since God has commanded her not to commit adultery. But in all other matters, she must obey, even when the decision does not seem wise.

This submission does not mean that she may not express her opinions. Quite to the contrary. She may disagree and press her arguments for her point of view with vigor—*so long as her attitude remains submissive.* When God designated a wife as her husband's **helper** (Genesis 2:18), He did not qualify that statement. She is to give him whatever help she can—including help in making family decisions. But, the help must truly be *help*; not nagging!

The husband, throughout this section, is said to be the one who must **love** (vv. 25,28,33). Never, in the Bible, is the wife commanded to love her husband. The inception of love, the maintenance of love and the growth of love are all the responsibility of the husband. Why? Because, as John says, "We (the church) love because He (Christ) first loved us (I John 4:19)." In this regard, we are to love **as Christ** gave Himself for His church (v. 25). How did He love? He **gave Himself**. Love begins with *giving*. Love your neighbor? Give to him. Love your enemy? Give him something to eat or drink. Love begins with the giving of one's self, one's possessions, or—whatever it is that one has that the one to be loved needs.

Christ wants to present His church without spot or wrinkle, as a chaste, beautiful bride on the wedding day. So should a husband. He should so help his wife to become what God wants that he does so. How? By following and using the Word (v. 26) in all his dealings with her.

30 we are members of His body.

31 **For this reason a man shall leave his father and mother and shall cleave to his wife and the two shall be one flesh.**

32 There is a great secret in this, but I am speaking about Christ and about the church.

33 Nevertheless, each one of you also must love his wife in the same way that he loves himself, and the wife must respect her husband.

He should love his wife as he does **his own body**. When he gets an injury in the body, he cares for it tenderly. So, too, should he **nourish and cherish** (two tender words in Greek and English) his wife as he does the injured limb. In doing so, he really cares for **himself** (v. 28[b]); if she is healthy and happy, he will be too, since they have entered into a relationship that means they are as one person (the meaning of **one flesh**). Paul acknowledges that not everything he says applies directly to the marriage relationship, as of course it does to Christ and his church, so he makes that point in verse 32. But, returning to it, he says, about the marriage relationship, let me sum it up this way: love your wife in the same way you already love your self, and, wives, respect (lit., fear) your husbands (v. 33). And, that is the sum of the matter: on the one hand loving leadership; on the other submissive respect.

This chapter, like the previous one, will be one to which you turn so often in counseling, the pages on which it is printed in your Bible will soon become excessively worn.

CHAPTER 6

---

1 Children, obey your parents in the Lord; this is right:
2 **Honor your father and your mother** (which is the first commandment with a promise:
3 **that it may go well for you, and that you may live long on the land**).

The second of the three authority/submission relationships appears at the beginning of the sixth chapter: the relationship of children to parents and parents to children. The relationship of the Christian with the state (an authoritative instrument of God according to I Peter; Romans) is not treated in this place. I suspect that this omission is purposeful. In these last three chapters Paul's concern is the Christian's walk *with other Christians*, as I pointed out previously. In discussing his walk in relationship to the state, Paul would be dealing with quite a different matter—the Christian's relationship to an unbelieving authority. But Ephesians is concerned with the relationships of believers *within* the Church.

The order of the three relationships is probably given in order of importance: marriage, family, work. Or, at least, in order of closeness and intimacy—which, of course, gives significance to them. The husband/wife relationship is permanent and the first, and foundational one, in creation. There can be no stable order where this relationship breaks down. The church, the state, etc., all depend on it. The parent/child relationship, though very important, is not intended to be permanent; the child must leave home and cleave to another more intimately than he ever could to his parents. Work, though important, may be temporary and even changing. At any rate, the counselor may suggest that the counselee think of these areas in order of importance. Work may not destroy family, family may not destroy marriage.

Children are to **obey their parents in the Lord**. Why? **This is right.** That is Paul's argument. To obey **in the Lord** means to obey as the Lord instructs, that is, according to biblical injunctions and examples. But why is it **right**? Because, as verse 2 makes clear, God commanded it in the children's commandment. Which, verses 2 and 3 also point out, is the commandment that has an incentive (promise) attached. And, naturally, the promise, turned inside out, says the opposite. What that means is that if one fails to obey his parents, things will not go well with him, and he may not live a long life of prosperity. That fact, every counselor may

4   Fathers, don't provoke your children to anger, but rather bring them up with the Lord's discipline and counsel.

5   Slaves, obey your lords according to the flesh with fear and trembling in singleness of heart, as you would obey Christ,

---

observe to youngsters in rebellion, is something to reckon with when they disobey God by disobeying their parents.

But the **promise** is an incentive. Children are motivated by promises; something else that must not escape the keen counselor. There is a difference, however, between a promise and a bribe. The latter involves accomplishing something quite easy for one to do, but that he does only to get some promised reward. The former is something he does that is difficult, yet he achieves it. This distinction should be carefully preserved. You will find it of the utmost importance in the discussion of child raising.

Well, that is the child's side. But verse 4 addressed the parents through the **father** (the one principally responsible for bringing up his children). It is possible by underdiscipline or overdiscipline to provoke children to anger so that they say in exasperation, "O, what's the use?" (for detailed information on this, see my book, *Christian Living in the Home*). Parents must avoid both extremes. Consistency, fairness, making the punishment fit the crime, etc., are all important. But, note, especially, the remainder of verse 4: **bring them up with the Lord's discipline and counsel.** That is to say, with the discipline and counsel that the Lord provides in His Word, and which He, Himself, exhibits toward His children in that same Word. The two words give a balanced approach. The first means discipline with teeth that sees that matters are done. The second has to do with instructing and teaching the child from the experiences of discipline. They correspond to the Proverb that teaches parents to discipline with the rod *and* reproof. Without one or the other, discipline fails— and provokes to anger. In counseling, look for failure on one side or the other. You will usually discover that the problems you encounter in the discipline of children may be accounted for by a failure to be strict enough while emphasizing tenderness, or not tender enough while emphasizing strictness. Both must be involved in discipline for it to be God's discipline. Notice, if you will, how in the prophets God speaks sharply when disciplining His errant children, but also how He talks tenderly to them through those same prophets. Prophetic discipline in the home will neglect neither.

Now, in verses 5-9. Paul takes up the third authority/submission rela-

6   but not only when they are watching you work, as people-pleasers do, but rather as slaves of Christ doing God's will from the soul,
7   serving as slaves with good will as for the Lord and not for people,
8   knowing that whatever good each one may do he will receive back from the Lord again, whether he is a slave or free.
9   Lords, do the same for them. Don't threaten, knowing that in the heavens is One Who is both Lord of them and of you, and there is no favoritism with Him.

---

tionship: that of **master and slave**. Addressing both as Christians, again, he is interested in their walk one with another. Beginning with **the slave** (the one who must submit is addressed first, as in both of the other relationships; cf. v. 5:22, 6:1), he says **obey your lords according to the flesh.** Again, obedience is combined with **fear** (or respect) **and trembling in singleness of heart as you would obey Chris**t. There is to be genuine respect for the authority of God in the workplace. Many counselees have problems with their work, fellow employees, their bosses, etc. They need to be pointed to this place as well as the parallel section in Colossians 2.

The one who is **lord according to the flesh** (or boss in this world) is to be *obeyed*. That is a hard concept for the present day worker to understand. It is almost part of the job description of today's worker that he must gripe and complain about his superiors, either openly or otherwise. Yet failure to follow Paul's injunction is a key reason *for* discontent on the job. When one works in a spirit of resentment and rebellion, he is working under stress. That, in time, will wear him down physically. And his attitude will become insufferable. Both are wrong. Obedience that is concerned lest it not be adequate (**fear and trembling** in Paul mean having a concern to do a good job and not "mess up," as we say) is what God requires. Moreover, singleness of heart—the opposite of half-heartedness is essential. It is the very lax way in which many work that is the cause of their discontent. The Christian is to do all things, even his work, to God's glory. He is to do it with all his might. The worker who works *only* to make money, but cares little about how he works—so long as the paycheck keeps coming—does not work with **singleness of heart**. Indeed, his heart is not in it. Here the standard for work is at the highest: work **as you would obey Christ**.

And, indeed, it is *He* for Whom you *are* working. That is why you can work just as well when the boss isn't watching as when he is — you know Christ sees and cares (v. 6)! And, so, you can work not just with an

10 Finally, be strong in the Lord and in the strength of His might.

11 Put on God's complete armor so that you can stand up against the devil's devices

12 (our conflict isn't against blood and flesh, but rather against rulers, against authorities, against world rulers of this darkness, and against the evil spiritual forces in the heavenly places).

13 For this reason take up God's complete armor, so that you may be able to resist in the evil day, and when it is all over you will still be standing.

---

outward show but with an inner (soul) commitment. Unless you work with the right inner attitude, therefore, the One for Whom you really work, Who (unlike your earthly boss) knows your inner spirit, is not pleased. And, even if the earthly boss fails to acknowledge your faithfulness, Christ knows and, in His time, will reward you for it (v. 8) because you work for Him (v. 7).

Then, Paul turns to Christian **lords**. They too are to do the same for their slaves: they are to be lords over them as Christ is over His people. Treat them all fairly, as your heavenly Lord treats every one of you, he says. Remember, you may be a "lord" here, but that cuts no ice with God. He shown no favoritism. You are His slave, and He expects you (in your position as lord of your slaves) to be a faithful slave for Him.

Counselees, having problems with work should be advised to make a study of the passage here. It is short enough for them to get out a couple of commentaries and go to work on it. It would do them good to have dug out these, and other facts, for themselves and will impress them on their minds for a long time to come—perhaps even to be remembered while at work either as a worker, an employer or manager.

Now, in verse 10, Paul begins to wind up this treatise. He says, **Finally, be strong in the Lord and in the strength of His might.** What he has been advocating will require more strength than the Christian possesses innately; it must be acquired from the Lord Himself. All God's commands are designed to drive us back to His Son for grace. That, in a sense, is the sum and substance of the Christian life: I am living for Christ according to His wisdom and by His strength. But His strength is entirely adequate.

Moreover, He provides armor for the battle (Christian living is, essentially, warfare). The key to understanding Paul's emphasis in verses 10-18, in which he exhorts us to be able to withstand the devil's attacks, is found in verses 11 and 13. In each he stresses the need to put on **God's complete armor**. It is the *completeness* to which he is calling us. If pieces

14 So then, stand, **tightening the belt of truth about your waist, putting on the breastplate of righteousness,**
15 and **protecting your feet with readiness to present the good news of peace**.

---

are missing, we become vulnerable in our battle against the spiritual forces in this world (v. 12). The devil and his hosts are able to successfully tempt us when we neglect one or more of these elements. What are they, and why is each important? And it is precisely that fact—that a counselee may have one or more pieces of equipment with which to wage successful warfare, but may have neglected others—for which the counselor must be on alert.

For instance, Paul begins with **truth** (v. 14). Now, if one knows little of what the Scriptures teach, he is extremely vulnerable. If he is ignorant of or despises truth, he will surely be laid low. Paul considers it so important that he places it at the head of the list. On this matter, see Jesus' words in John 17:17. One of the tasks of a biblical counselor is to correct error, meet ignorance head on and impart truth to his counselees. Check out the truth-possession level of each counselee. If you find it very low, or too low to deal with the issues that are uppermost in the counseling case, then, before progressing further, work on this matter. In fighting the battles of the Lord, truth is uppermost.

Then, of course, Paul notes the importance of **righteousness** (I say "of course," because the Scriptures always emphasize how utterly crucial it is not only to know truth, but also to live in accordance with it). If your counselee is one who knows much truth, but it is all intellectualized, not life-actualized, he will definitely need help in bringing truth to bear on daily decision-making. Life is action. It is a series of moment by moment decisions that we make either for or against Jesus Christ. If a counselee does not know how to bring truth into a fruitful relationship to life, he will fall in the battle and not remain standing at the end of the day (vv. 13,14).

There is a need for protecting one's feet. It is interesting that this is said to be **a readiness to present the good news of peace**. In other words, a good defense is a good offense. Presenting the gospel to others in evangelism is one way to overcome the wiles of the devil. Pushing back his minions means less ability on their part to wage an attack. Any counselee who is not evangelizing whenever he can fails to protect himself and others from the attacks of the enemy. While it is true that a counselee may not have a very good witness because of his failures and sins, neverthe-

16 Along with all of that take up the shield of faith that will enable you to put out all of the evil one's flaming darts,

17 and take the **helmet of salvation** and the Spirit's sword, which is God's Word.

18 Do all of this with prayer and petition, praying at all times by the Spirit, and to that end stay alert with all perseverance and petition concerning all of the saints.

---

less, by confessing these and getting on with Christian living, even he can win a hearing from the lost. Perhaps the change he makes in counseling itself can be the attraction for others to listen to the message. Do not let him think for a minute that he is done for as a witness for Christ just because he got into difficulty. As he emerges, one of the things he should do is to take advantage of the change to speak to others about how Christ made the difference. However, you must make sure that the change sticks before you encourage him to begin to talk to others about it.

Faith is a shield (v. 16). It will help you ward off the flaming darts of the evil one. In proportion to the faith that one has is his strength. How is faith strengthened in counseling? By learning, believing and acting on beliefs from the Bible. Counselors should encourage counselees to step out in faith according to the directions and promises of the Scriptures. This may begin by small increments with reference to lesser items, but may soon progress to much larger ones.

Of course, you will be killed in the battle if your head is not protected by **salvation**. I have said much about the fact that it is impossible to counsel an unbeliever. He doesn't have the resources to make the changes that please God (cf. Romans 8:8). The whole enterprise is hopeless apart from this *sin qua non*.

Finally, one must be able to use the Scriptures as a **sword**. This sword, note carefully, is the *Spirit's* sword, not the counselee's. Too often, the counselee gets the idea that it is he who can fight the battle in his power and skill so long as he uses the Bible. But, the Scriptures, used only in the power of the counselee, will have little or no effect. The tool, ministered by the counselee, in the **Spirit's** power, however, is the most powerful weapon ever known. That is why it is crucial to put on each piece **with prayer** (v. 18), asking God the Spirit to work.

Alertness on the part of the counselee is also crucial. He must be ever ready for the attacks of the enemy. It is also important for him to continue to fight to the end; he must learn not to give up, but to **persevere**. And, he must pray for other Christians who are involved in the fight.

19 Pray for me that I may be given the right words to say when I open my mouth to make known the secret of the good news boldly
20 (for which I am an ambassador with a chain), that I may speak boldly, as indeed I should.
21 Now, that you may know all about me, and what I am doing, Tychicus, the dear brother and faithful servant in the Lord, will tell you everything.

All in all, one would be hard put to attempt to find a program more adequately fitted to the needs of the average counselee. Surely these verses concerning the Christian's complete armor, then, will become a standby in the repertoire of every wise counselor. But, because it is essential to remember the fact, let me emphasize how important it is to check out *each* counselee on *every one* of these elements. It he is missing any, or very deficient in some, that is where the enemy is sure to attack and gain a victory. Stress the need for **completeness**. And, the list actually could be used as a check list in those instances where failure has occurred.

The conclusion of the treatise is found in the last six verses (vv. 19-24). If Paul is not beyond asking his readers to pray for him in his work, why should you be? One of the assignments you can write on the weekly assignment sheet for a counselee may be to pray for you. Paul knew what was required of him, he asked others to pray that God would give him what he needed (in this case **boldness**). Counseling, like preaching, requires boldness. If you find that boldness is a lack in your work, then it might also be a request you would make to your counselee. Or, are you not bold enough even to make this request!? Think about that one for a while

Tychicus, who was probably carrying this letter to its recipients, would report on what the Lord was doing through Paul and how the ministry was progressing while he was in jail. He would also be the bearer of encouragement (vv. 21,22). Then comes the final words of benediction to all whose **love** is God-given (Cf. Romans 5:5) and, therefore, genuine; no other sort of love is **incorruptible**. It is the love mentioned, along with God-given **faith**, in verse 23 about which Paul writes.

Well, you have traversed the treatise called the Letter to the Ephesians. It is a powerfully important one for the Christian counselor. Don't you find it so? If not, then perhaps there is something wrong with your counseling approach. Why else would this important treatise not impress you with its counseling resources and directives as well as examples? I am not saying that my commentary should impress you, but surely, if you

22   I sent him to you for this very purpose, that you may learn all about us, and that he may encourage your hearts.

23   Peace to the brothers, and love with faith from God the Father and from the Lord Jesus Christ.

24   Help be with all those who love our Lord Jesus with an incorruptible love.

---

have pursued it at all, some important issues must have arisen in your thinking—unless, as I said, your approach is one in which the Bible fails to figure very largely, if at all. For those who have benefited from thinking about the counseling values of the letter, please remember that the commentary I have provided is limited. Why not use the margins of this book as a place to record additional counseling insights as they occur to you? Then, together with those printed here, you will have a source to which you may wish to turn again and again in order to inform and inspire you.

Ephesians is a book on counseling—*par excellence!*

Introduction to
Colossians

The *Book of Colossians* is a letter paralleling much of the material in the treatise we call "Ephesians." The one, in many places, helps to interpret the other. They, therefore, ought to be studied in tandem. Though there are many similarities, there are differences; one is not a copy—even in part—of the other. In Ephesians, Paul emphasizes the Church (never to the detriment of its Head) while in Colossians he emphasizes the Head (never to the exclusion of the Church). But the emphases *do* differ. In Ephesians the stress is on the unity of the church, while in Colossians the stress falls on the deity of Jesus Christ.

In Colossians, which is more of a letter than a treatise, Paul has many things to say that ought to be of great interest to the counselor. The book deals with a Gnostic heresy that had a legalistic, Jewish background. While many think that the gnosticism was not yet full blown, it would seem, rather, that Paul is dealing not with something which is incipient but with a system already well-defined. He does not write as someone trying to counter something vague, but rather, a viewpoint that had already taken on the form of a movement with its doctrines, principles and practices articulated, and, therefore, subject to definite analysis and detailed discussion. The problem may lie not so much in the fact that the system was not yet fully shaped but that our knowledge of its origins and viewpoints *at this period* are deficient. Certainly, later on, we do find full-fledged teaching, in systematic form, that corresponds very nicely to what we read here. At any rate, the book deals with the problem of this Jewish Gnosticism that, providentially, every counselor may be thankful for since, as a result, the apostle Paul was forced to deal in depth with subjects to which, elsewhere, he but alludes.

CHAPTER 1

1 Paul, an apostle of Christ Jesus by God's will, and Timothy our brother,

2 to the saints and faithful brothers in Christ in Colossae:
May help and peace from God our Father be yours.

The introductory words of the Book are not exceptional. Paul identifies himself and Timothy as the writers who are, successively, an **apostle** and a **brother**. There is, seemingly, no stress on either fact. The letter is addressed to the **saints and faithful brothers in Christ** who are in Colossae. The insertion of the word **faithful** does distinguish those who have maintained the faith from those who have gone over to the heresy. God is concerned with faithfulness in His people. Counselees should not be given the idea that He looks upon all members of the church alike. Sometimes when we stress (rightly) the fact that no one is better than the other and that God is no respecter of persons, people extrapolate those ideas to mean that it doesn't matter what you are like; God will look on each one in the same way. As the letters to the seven churches of Revelation clearly indicate God not only deals with churches as such on a different basis, according to their faithfulness or lack of it, but also distinguishes groups and individuals within them.

The **saints** are God's "set apart ones." They have been set apart from the rest of mankind to worship, love and serve Him. When they do not do so faithfully, they should be concerned. Biblical counseling should always maintain an atmosphere that accords with this concern. The counseling emphasis should never principally focus on what the counselee gets from counseling, but on a joint effort to glorify God's Name by enabling the counselee to serve Him more faithfully. What the counselee gets out of counseling must always be secondary—a by-product. That is not always easy to do. Counselees come, usually, not viewing themselves as unfaithful saints but as persons with individual problems. They usually focus on self. The first, and perhaps most important, service the counselor can render is to change the atmosphere in which the counseling takes place. What he wants is a sense of united effort on the part of both counselee and counselor to help make the counselee fit to serve Him more faithfully—whatever the problem may be (heresy, as in this case, or some other thing). At any rate, from the outset, Paul's concern is to help these Colossians become more faithful.

3 We always thank God, the Father of our Lord Jesus Christ, when we pray for you,
4 since we have heard of your faith in Christ Jesus and the love that you have toward all the saints,

---

They are not saints because of anything in them, but only because of the grace of God. They have no intrinsic power to change or to serve faithfully. Therefore, they need **help and peace** from the Father (v. 2^b).

In verses 3-6 Paul pens a thanksgiving that is filled with instructional material, much of which is quite appropriate for counselors. He says that he faithfully prays for them, whenever he prays (v. 3) What an assurance! It is not wrong for a counselor also to let his counselees know that he will be praying for them. But, he may also point out from verses 3,4, that his prayer is a prayer of thanksgiving that is based on the love they have for other saints. The counselor may not honestly be able to pray that prayer of thanksgiving. Yet, he can tell his counselee that he is looking forward to the day when he can. What is a reality to Paul can be a hope for you and your counselee.

It was their **faith in Christ Jesus** that made it possible for them to extend love toward all the saints (v. 4). And, of course, it was not just the saving faith they exercised but the growing faith that they placed in Christ that enabled them to love others. If there are problems your counselees have with regard to loving other Christians (perhaps each other, for that matter), their difficulty, among other things, may be the smallness of their faith. After all, if one doubts whether there is any possibility for change in a relationship that has gone sour, how well will he work and pray for change? In such cases, doubt in the promises or power of God may have to be confronted. Usually, this doubt will not appear for what it is. It will be expressed as doubt about the *other person,* not about God or His Word. You, therefore, must clarify the situation, setting it forth for what it really is—doubt that God, through His Word can change another. You may have to say something like this: "So, you don't think that Marge can change?" That's right. "Then, what you are really saying is that God can't change her, right?" No, I'm saying *she* doesn't want to change, or can't. "No, you are saying *God* doesn't want to or can't." How do you get that? "Thought you'd never ask! I get it this way. The Bible makes it abundantly clear that any changes *we* make on our own are worthless. It is God Who must change us if we are to change in ways that please Him. Biblical change is the fruit of the Spirit. So, in talking about the change God wants, change

5   because of the hope that is laid up for you in the heavens. You heard
before about this in the Word of truth concerning the good news,

---

that He alone can effect by His Spirit, you are saying that this isn't possible; that means you are saying God won't or can't change Marge. Right?"
Hmmmmm.

Such faith is based on **the hope that is laid up for you in the heavens**. The word "hope" in the Bible means "expectation" or "anticipation," never a doubtful thing. It is something for which the believer hopes because it has not yet happened; but it is as certain as if it had since this hope is firmly rooted in God's biblical promises. It is the hope of eternal life with God Himself. It is the hope that one day we shall be entirely free from sin and all its misery. The believer's hope, then, is the basis for his faith in God's promises for this life. If God will provide all that in eternity, surely He will provide for the small needs of this life. If the greater, then surely the lesser.

And, of course, this was the hope that they heard about in the gospel from the beginning (v. 5^b). The message of truth was the good news of eternal salvation and all that means. Surely, counselees need to be brought back again and again to the gospel of Christ. In no other place will they find true hope and such encouragement.

This hope is as sure as God Himself—it is laid up in the heavens. That is to say, God in heaven is guarding and keeping it ready for the day when you will receive it. And the same God Who does that is the God Who provides now. So, love and faith growingly are possible if one realizes the implications of the hope (expectation) that he has in the gospel. Never get very far away from the good news itself. Everything worthwhile in counseling is possible because of the death and resurrection of Christ.

They had **heard about** the heavenly hope before when they heard and believed the **gospel** (v. 5). The anticipation of the eternal inheritance is, naturally, an essential part of the good news. The message is not merely that one's sins may be forgiven, but also that one may spend eternity with Jesus Christ, clothed not only in His *imputed* righteousness, but also in a perfect righteousness that is *imparted* as well. What one looks forward to with hope is important to how he lives here. If he longs for righteousness, not merely for its personal blessings, but because it pleases his Lord, that will influence his goals and desires today. It is important, then, to help counselees acquire proper hope. If that hope is distorted, or if one has replaced it with a lesser one, there may be need to revitalize it.

6   that came to you as also in the whole world it is bearing fruit and
growing in the same way that it has among you from the day that you heard
and truly knew God's grace.

The good news that came to them, was bearing fruit and growing
throughout the world. What Paul was preaching was the universal message that was spreading everywhere (note the preponderance of all-inclu-
sive terms throughout this first chapter). Paul, unlike those who were
propounding the heresy about which he is going to warn, preached a message in accord with that which the other apostles proclaimed. It was no
esoteric system, confined to some local area. That was part of Augustine's
argument against heretics in his day: the truth can never be something that
is adapted only to one people or country. The scope of Jesus' Great Commission was worldwide. That argument may be of use to remember whenever a counselee is caught up in (or tempted to espouse) some narrow,
unusual belief-system. Certainly it is pertinent to the counselee who wants
to know why you are telling him that he should do such and such. The
answer is "Because that is what the Bible teaches, and that has been the
practice of Christ's church throughout the ages in accordance with the
Bible."

Like a productive plant, the gospel has spread and propagated itself
(v. 6), just as it did among the Colossians. They had heard and truly
known the grace of God. Again and again a counselor must stress the
importance of the fact that all that we have that is pleasing to Christ is the
result of grace. We have not earned our salvation or the favor of God. He,
in spite of our sin, saved us solely because of His grace. And, in all our
failures as believers He continues to work with us by grace. An understanding of grace places the emphasis on what God does, not on the supposed worth of the counselee. It is God Who should be honored for any
good that is attained or anything fine that is accomplished. Focusing on
God and His gracious working keeps the counselee from comparing himself with others. He never has the right to boast. He must ever give thanks
to God and not take credit for himself. What I am saying is that the word
grace ought to be heard frequently in the counseling room. It is the
answer to many problems found there.

Possibly it was Epaphras who first brought the gospel to the Colossian Church which, it seems, was not one that Paul himself began (though
he knew many persons—Philemon, *et al.*—in it); cf. 2:1. Epaphras seems
to have been Paul's contact with the congregation and the congregation's

7   You learned this from Epaphras, our dear fellow slave, who is Christ's faithful servant for us,

8   who also has clearly pointed out to us your love by the Spirit.

9 So, from the day that we heard about it, we haven't stopped praying for you and asking that you may be filled with the full knowledge of His will in all spiritual wisdom and understanding

---

principal contact with Paul (vv. 7,8). He brought a message that was faithfully proclaimed. It is authentic and true Paul says; trust it. And, he has made known the congregation's love, which is the fruit of the Spirit (v. 8).

All-in-all, Epaphras comes off here as a tried and true friend and worker in the ministry of the Word. These are high words of praise. But, note, even in this case, grace is uppermost: what he has done and the results of his labor among the Colossians, are attributed ultimately to the Holy Spirit (**by the Spirit**).

Paul has mentioned his prayers for the Church (vv. 3,4). Now, he further expresses the contents of those prayers. He asks God that they may have full knowledge, wisdom to use it properly as it issues in a life-style that pleases Christ and fortitude to withstand and endure trial in patience. That is one mouthful. Yet, think of it! Paul's prayers are comprehensive. He wants nothing but the best for them; and he wants it in completeness—across the board. What Paul desires for his readers is what every counselor should wish to see in his counselees, and for which he should ask God for the ability to help them find it.

Look at a couple of those items found in verses 9-11. First, notice that Paul continually prayed for these things (v. 9). That he *regularly* asked for them is what he means by not having **stopped praying**. The first item is that they **may be filled with the full knowledge of His will**. The prayer is basic. Every counselee must know God's will for him in his difficulties. And, if he does not, it is the counselor's task to pray that he will, and to assist him, so far as it is practicable to do so, to come to this knowledge. God's will is found but one place—in God's Word. It is the counselor's duty, therefore, to help a counselee to study, understand, faithfully acquiescence in and apply it to his life. That is a large task; but it is a large prayer. One of the principal needs of many counselees is to understand the will of God *in his situation*. That is where much confusion arises. Having once come to a **full** understanding of God's will in some matter, many times the problem is more than half solved. The prayer is on target. After all, this knowledge was the real need; not some kind of *gno-*

135

10 to walk in a way that is worthy of the Lord, pleasing Him in everything, bearing the fruit of every sort of good work and growing in the full
knowledge of God.

11 May you be empowered with every sort of power that is in keeping
with His glorious might that with joy you may fully endure and learn to be
completely patient,

---

sis (Greek word for knowledge, from which "Gnosticism," the claim to
special knowledge, comes).

Again, as verse 9 indicates, wisdom to use this knowledge with
understanding is what the Spirit gives. But also, again, He does not do so
immediately; He works mediately, in and through His Word. The Holy
Spirit is peculiarly related to the Bible. It is His Book; He moved men to
write it. Now that He has completed the process, He does not abandon the
Bible, but uses it as the means by which He works in the lives of believers.
So, once more, we are thrown back on the Bible and the Spirit. The prayer
is that the Spirit will thus enable them to be **filled** (dominated; cf. Ephesians 5:18) with all **wisdom and understanding**.

When one has the sort of knowledge that issues in wisdom and
understanding he is able to **walk in a way that is worthy of the Lord** and
that pleases Him (v. 10). This is the goal of the Christian's life: to please
His Lord Who died for him. Never let the counselee lose sight of this.
And, help him to see that this is the way in which he manifests that pleasing walk: by **bearing fruit of every sort of good work**. Interestingly,
Paul conceives of this growth in the Christian's life as a cyclical thing.
When one begins to acquire fuller knowledge of God's will (v. 9), thus
enabling him to walk more fully in accordance with His desires, this, in
turn, helps him to gain further knowledge of God (v. 10). And, in counseling, that insight is very important. Whenever a counselee takes a step forward, that enables him to take other steps as well. Therefore, it is not
always so important which thing he does first (though order is sometimes
critical); just that he does something to please Christ according to His
will. No matter how small and seemingly insignificant, that having been
achieved, will not only strengthen him, but it will give him further insight
into the nature of God Himself.

But, power is also important. And, the Spirit's power, given to enable
him to endure with patience the vicissitudes of this life, in ways appropriate to the glorious might of God Himself, is also available. It is the power
not only to withstand, but to withstand patiently **with joy**. If there are two

12 thanking the Father, Who has made you fit for your share of the inheritance of the saints in light.

13 He rescued us from the dominion of darkness and brought us instead into the empire of His dear Son,

14 in whom we have redemption—the forgiveness of sins.

---

characteristics lacking in many counselees it is patience and joy. The anger, discouragement, impatience with others that so often characterize them is all too apparent. To mention joy in the midst of trial seems almost obscene to the modern Christian. He is so caught up in his own rights that he thinks little of how the Lord is working out His great plan in his life. Yet, to be patient for God to answer prayer—especially in regard to the conduct of others—and to remain joyful throughout difficulties (knowing that all is working together for good) is essential to the solution of many counselee problems. The verse, coupled with those that precede, is a useful counseling tool.

And, in his prayers for the Colossians, Paul thanks God that they are in the process of being made **fit** for their share of the heavenly inheritance. To administer properly the inheritance that is coming to each of the saints of God, one must be fit. In the kingdom of light to which they are called, they must have what it takes (that is the meaning of the word "fit") to engage in the tasks to which God has called them. Presumably, then, He is preparing us even now for tasks that we will be pursuing there and then. We have been rescued from the dominion of darkness (Satan's kingdom of ignorance, error and death) and brought into the empire of God's dear Son, Jesus Christ; it is a realm of light (knowledge, truth and life). This happened, of course, by the redemption that He effected, namely, the forgiveness of our sins (vv. 12-14). Since Christ has redeemed us, freeing us from the authority of Satan, it is possible to become fit for the work of His eternal kingdom. And, because the deliverance is already in effect (you are rescued from Satan's authority and you are already part of the empire of the King of Kings), you need not wait until death to begin preparing for the tasks that lie ahead. We do not now know what they will be but, in part, it seems, they will be allocated according to the ways counselees do or do not become fit to pursue them. That in itself should be a strong incentive to shape up, regardless of what others do or don't do. You are fitting yourself for tasks in the eternal kingdom of light.

Now, having referred to Jesus Christ as the One Who brought us redemption, Paul goes on to discuss His person in a powerful paragraph

15 He is the Image of the invisible God, the First-born Who is over all creation,

16 since by Him, all things visible and invisible in the heavens and on the earth were created; regardless of whether they are thrones, or dominions, or rulers, or authorities, all things were created through Him and for Him.

17 He is before all things and by Him all things hold together.

---

that encompasses verses 15-20. In this section of the letter, He is concerned to set forth the truths about Christ that would offset the Gnostic heresy that attacked His deity. He, Paul says, in his initial sally, is **the Image of the invisible God, the First-born Who is over all creation** (v. 15). That is a remarkable sentence, profound in its teachings and implications. In it is the contrast between the *invisibility* of God the Father and the Image (Greek: *eikon*, a *visible representation*) that Christ is. Jesus Christ is the Medium by which the invisible Father is manifested to men. But the divine can be pictured only by the divine; anything less would be a false representation. Jesus is that exact representation. As He walked on earth, He was Immanuel, "God with us." He said, "he that has seen Me has seen the Father (John 14:9)."

He is also the Firstborn, Who is over all creation. It does not say "First-created." That is precisely the notion Paul is taking pains to refute. But "Firstborn." In Jewish writings, Jehovah, Himself, has the epithet applied to Him. Nothing in it must be understood to diminish His deity or eternal nature. It is a word having to do with Hebrew rights and prerogatives of primogeniture. The firstborn was the prominent one, who wielded authority and power. He was accorded first place. So, here, the ideas of preeminence, power, and principal place are uppermost. Christ was being demoted to some lesser position by the errorists. Paul wants the reader to think of Christ as before and above all others. His position of authority makes Him Head over all creation.

And why not? After all, it was by Him that all things were created, —all things (visible and invisible) and all creatures (enumerated in v. 16). And, he tops off this magnificent statement of His utter preeminence by saying not only were all things created **by** Him but also **for** Him. Such a thing could be said of no one less than God Himself.

Verse 17 strengthens the description of His deity. He was not a part of creation, but existed before it. He not only brought all things into existence, but in Him, all things consist (or hold together). His deity was manifested not only in creation, but also at the present time. As God, He is the

18   He is the Head of the body, the church; He is the Originator, the First-
born from the dead that in everything He might be preeminent.
19   God was pleased to dwell in Him in all His fullness,

One Who sustains creation. Without His willing its existence, creation
would disappear into nothingness. He is the Sustainer as well as the Creator of the universe. What greater could be said of Him?

And, after this theological discourse (important to refute the heretics), Paul now applies what he has said to the Church. Jesus, as Head
over all things, is also Head over His church (v. 18), here (working the figure out) called His **body**.

He is the **Originator, Firstborn from the dead** as well. Paul seems
to be heaping up superlatives. He refers to Jesus by the highest titles he
can muster. In everything—even the resurrection from the dead—He must
be given the first place. Why? **That in everything He might be preeminent.**

And, God was dwelling in Him **in all His fullness:** He was fully, not
partially (or anything else that might diminish His full deity) divine. And,
in the grand plan of redemption, God was effecting the reconciliation of
all that had been marred by sin. His cross made peace with God, as He
paid the sufficient penalty for the sins of His people and bought back all
things that had been lost in the fall, so that the elect as well as the groan-
ing creation alike will be reconciled to God.

Your counselee is caught up in something powerful, something
grand, something greater than himself and his problems. What Jesus is
doing in his life is part of this grand drama of redemption that is being
played out before the entire universe. As angels, and whatever other creatures there may be, watch, what is transpiring in his life is part of a grand
demonstration of the nature and the purposes of God (see my book, *The
Grand Demonstration*, for more on this). Give counselees this kind of a
picture and they will be able to look on their problems with joy and
patience. Seldom does the discussion in a counseling session soar to such
heights. But it should.

In verse 19, the word *pleroma* ("fullness") is used. Doubtless, this
was a reference to the heresy which used this word as a significant term in
its theology. Paul identified the **fullness** with no one other than Jesus
Christ Himself. Anyone who tries to find help in living this life outside
the realm of Christ and His Word places himself in jeopardy. Like the heretics who said that Jesus and the Spirit were not enough, but that to have

20 and through Him to reconcile to Himself all things, whether they are things on the earth or things in the heavens, making peace by the blood of His cross.

21 You too at one time were estranged and enemies in your minds, involved in evil works.

22 But now He has reconciled you in His fleshly body through his death to present you holy and blameless and irreproachable before Him,

---

further knowledge and the fullness of which Jesus was only one part (an aeon), they boarder on denying to Christ all that He is and can do. Paul is clearly concerned about any system that would place Christ on a level with anyone or anything else. He does not wish to share the place and power of Christ with anyone else; He stands alone. He alone is the answer. The same is true of counseling. Nothing else was necessary to redeem us from our sin and bring forgiveness to us than the blood of the cross. So, too, nothing more is necessary than the full knowledge and power of the Lord and the Spirit to enable us to become fit to serve in the heavenly kingdom. Eclectics, take heed.

Verses 21-23 bring this theological teaching down to practical life. Before coming to Christ as Savior, the Colossians were **estranged** from God, His people and His kingdom. Indeed, this estrangement meant not only alienation but enmity in their thinking, which, inevitably, involved them in evil works. Now, that does not mean that every unbeliever goes around thinking how he may fight God (though some do). What Paul is describing is a **mind** oriented toward self and sin rather than toward God and righteousness. What the unbeliever likes and appreciates and strives to obtain is contrary to what God approves. Therein is the enmity. The unbeliever, if pressed, will always come out in favor of what is wrong, thus showing himself to belong to that kingdom of darkness which is opposed to God's kingdom. Whenever he contributes anything to the progress of the devil's domain, at the same time he (usually unwittingly) contributes to that which opposes God. Therein is the enmity manifested.

That was true **at one time** of Paul's readers (v. 21). But no longer. Now, being reconciled by the offering of the body of Christ as a sacrifice for their sin, He is working at presenting them holy and blameless before the Father at His coming. Again, these are words for counselees. Blame-worthiness and unholiness; those are two of the things encountered regularly in the counseling room. And they are two things every biblical counselor is concerned to deal with. He wants to be able to assist in the process by which counselees will be presented to the Father **irreproach-**

23 if, indeed, you continue grounded and stable in the faith and are not moved away from the hope of the good news that you heard, that has been preached to every creature under the sun, and of which I, Paul, became a servant.

24 I am now glad about my sufferings for you, and in my flesh I am filling up the remainder of Christ's afflictions on behalf of His body which is the church,

---

able. Like Paul, who was writing for this very purpose, the wise counselor counsels for no lesser purpose. And this will happen (at least to some extent) if they remain **grounded and stable in the faith**. As we have seen, there were forces at work trying to shake that faith, just as there are usually contrary forces at work in the counselee's life. But counselees must remain true to the faith of the gospel, the one that is preached universally, the one for which God raised up Paul to be a minister (v. 23). Again, there is the contrast between local gnosticism and the universal faith of the Church.

Paul now wants to discuss his sufferings on behalf of the gentile churches. He is **glad** to suffer if it will benefit them (words that are a far cry from the whining that counselees so often exhibit in the counseling room). It seems that we live in an era with quite a different ethos; today, there is such self-centeredness that even the slightest call to put one's self out for another seems to be too much! But, as he continues (v. 24), Paul discloses the even deeper motivation behind the extraordinary sufferings that he bore for the Churches (Cf. II Corinthians 6,11). He considered his suffering for the gospel to be a continuation of the suffering that Christ experienced. What does that mean? It means that just as he was persecuting not only the Church, but Jesus Christ, when headed to Damascus (Acts 9:4,5), now that he was suffering for the gospel's sake, his sufferings were in the same sense persecution aimed ultimately at Jesus Himself. As Head of His Church, His body, Jesus was the actual target whenever any member of His church was attacked.

If counselees who suffer in behalf of the gospel can only be helped to see things as Paul did, they would be willing to endure hardship as good soldiers of Jesus Christ, willing to suffer for Him and His Church. Counseling often needs to strike this note. I realize it is out of accord with the flabby mentality of many in the Church today, but, perhaps, it is precisely the antidote to that enfeebling, Caspar Milquetoast attitude.

Paul considers his ministry a stewardship handed to him by God. It is not a job or a profession. Professionalism (not in the good sense of com-

25 (of which I became a servant by God's stewardship, which was given to me for you to fulfill the Word of God),
26 the secret that has been hidden from ages and generations, but now has appeared to His saints,
27 those to whom, God wished to make known what is the riches of the glory of this secret among the Gentiles, which is Christ in you, the hope of glory,
28 Whom we announce, counseling every person and teaching every person as wisely as possible, so that we may present every person mature in Christ.

---

petence, but) in the sense of cold, impersonal, mechanical approaches to ministry is a major problem with biblical counselors today. They have taken a leaf from Freud and others who kept themselves distant from the counselee. Paul, who wept with those who wept and rejoiced with those who rejoiced (Romans 12:15) saw his work as quite personal. He was to serve God's Church by giving himself. This stewardship of the gospel, he told the Colossians, was **for you to fulfill the Word of God**. That meant that he saw his work not as something he did for his own benefit, but for the benefit of Christ's people by spreading the message from God as widely as possible (v. 25[b]). The apostles certainly were not career-minded

Paul's message was not merely the gospel, but, in addition, the fact that God had admitted Gentiles into the Church in exactly the same way as Jews, namely, on the basis of faith. There were obscure hints of this possibility in the Old Testament. Now that Paul had been commissioned as the apostle to the Gentiles he fought for the complete equality of believing Gentiles and Jews (See Galatians 1-4). Through him, largely, this truth was being made known to his generation as it had not been in ages past (v. 26).

God wanted His people (the "saints") to know about the riches of the eternal glory of heaven in the Kingdom of light. What was the secret, now disclosed? That Christ is **among** the Gentiles (probably the correct translation, rather than "in you" [gentiles]) as He is among believing Jews. They, too, could anticipate and eagerly look forward to this heavenly glory.

That was why Paul announced the coming and death of Christ (v. 28), and then counseled and taught each person who believed **as wisely as he could**. Counseling (*nouthesia*) and teaching (*didasko*) were the two sides of his ministry (for more, see Acts 20). He engaged fully in both. It is a serious mistake to separate them (Cf. Acts 20:20, 31). The two com-

29   For this I labor, struggling for it with all the energy that He so powerfully produces in me.

---

plement one another. And, only by coupling them can one hope to **present** each individual **mature in Christ**. Note the individual concern in
these verses. It is not only saints in general about which Paul concerned
himself, but **each one** of them. Too often, ministry is to the crowd. Counseling individualizes it. One of the benefits of counseling is, of course, the
ability to apply general truths, that one preaches broadcast, in specific
ways that meet the particulars of individual situations. And, Paul was so
committed to this sort of work that he said he **labored** (to the point of
exhaustion) at it. He struggled, exerting all the energy that God gave him
to do so (v. 29). There is a picture of counseling (as well as preaching) for
every counselor to emulate!

CHAPTER 2

1 Indeed, I want you to know how great a struggle I have on behalf of you and those who are in Laodicea, and on behalf of those who haven't seen my face in the flesh:

Paul continues the emphasis of the last chapter. He had spoken of his sufferings and his struggle in behalf of the Gentile churches. He noted how his ministry was concerned with teaching and counseling (which he inseparably links) of a sort designed to present individuals complete in Christ. Now, he reemphasizes the fact that he endured much for the Gentile churches in order to save them from Judaistic legalism by preserving their freedom of the gospel in Christ. Even though most of those in the church of Colossae, like those in nearby Laodicea, had not known him, Paul had worked hard for both churches. This was true of his general struggles to preserve the gospel, but referred particularly to the instruction he gave to those who worked in the midst of these two specific congregations. He says, "I now wish I could come directly to help combat this heretical intrusion into your membership, but, being in prison, I can't (v. 5). Nevertheless, I still want to encourage you by this letter, so that, in unity, all of your hearts may alike be filled with love for God, for one another and for me. If I can help in any way, I hope to encourage you to join together in love that leads to the wealth that belongs to a full assurance of understanding."

Notice how, once more, Paul strongly stresses the need for the type of theological understanding that leads to full assurance of the truth—as opposed to error that doesn't. When a counselee lacks assurance that is based on an understanding of truth, no amount of reassurance and encouragement from others will suffice. You cannot do for him what only he can do: namely avail himself of the knowledge and understanding that give assurance of the faith as the result of careful, personal study of Scripture. It is absolutely necessary, therefore, as an element of counseling, to get counselees into the study of the Bible in a substantial way as quickly as possible. This is particularly necessary when you suspect that the truth or falsity of some question may lie behind his problems. A counselee who thinks that certain sins may lead to a loss of his salvation, for instance, needs to study the pertinent passages on the subject. You can do little to solve the problems that grow out of this faulty understanding until it is

2　that their hearts may be encouraged as they are joined together in love, leading to all of the riches of a full assurance of understanding, that in turn results in a full knowledge of God's mystery, that is, Christ,

3　in Whom are hidden all of the treasures of wisdom and knowledge.

4　I say this that nobody may mislead you with plausible-sounding arguments.

---

corrected. It is such a concern that underlies what Paul is saying in this place.

The mystery, revealed, in this portion of Scripture, Paul tells us, is Christ Himself (v. 2). That does not mean Christ is mysterious, but that when He came many things that had been obscure or misunderstood about Him and His mission were not cleared up. The Old Testament saints looked for the coming of the Messiah, but they lacked knowledge about Him. Here, in contrast to the Colossian heretics, Christ is said to possess **all the treasures of wisdom and knowledge** (v. 3). The heretics saw Christ as one among many semi-divine beings, all of whom were on the same level. He was thought to be some sort of demiurge, not the Son of the living God. But, now that the mystery about the Messiah has been fully revealed at His coming, we see that not only were the heretics in error, but many of the expectations of the Old Testament saints were deficient as well. Now He is seen as the One in Whom God laid up (that's what **hidden** means) all the wealth of wisdom and knowledge that God Himself has. And, says Paul, by way of explanation, I am pointing this out so that these heretics may not **mislead** you into thinking that Christ is something less than He really is (v. 4). After all, they can be convincing when they use **arguments** that at first (before you think them through biblically) sound **plausible** (v. 4).

Paul is warning his readers. Counselors sometimes fail to warn about the potential dangers they see ahead. Paul was not like that. In Acts 20, for instance, when he takes leave of the Ephesian elders, he warns them that from the outside and from within, wolves in sheep's clothing will seek to devour the flock. Here he warns about seemingly plausible arguments. Do the same whenever you see potential dangers (of whatever sort) lying ahead of your counselees ("Now, when you leave here and go home, you may very well encounter persons who will want you to...").

Well, Paul couldn't be with them to help fight the battle against error. But, he wants them to know, he is with them **in spirit**. It is as if he could actually be there and observe what is happening: he is **delighted** to see

145

5   If, indeed, I am absent in the flesh, nevertheless I am with you in spirit, delighted to see your good order and the firmness of your faith in Christ.

6 So then, as you have received Christ Jesus the Lord, walk in Him,

---

their **good order and the firmness of their faith**. From the reports he received, he could gain a fairly accurate picture of what was happening. To encourage the Church to continue in its present way of dealing with the heresy, he tells them of his delight over the firm stand they had taken thus far. How important to encourage those who have done well by telling them so and letting them know of your pleasure at their successes for Christ! Do you? Or do you don the white coat, never letting the counselee know your personal response to his efforts?

Good order (a concern of Paul in several letters: cf. II Thessalonians 3) is of importance. Disorder in the churches accounted for much failure in doctrine. People who are unstable, who can't be counted on to stand for their faith, will soon fall for something else. No wonder, then, that he was delighted to hear of (he could almost **see**) their **firmness**. When you discover firmness in faith in a counselee, rejoice. You are on the right track.

Continue in the same way, says Paul: **as you have received Christ Jesus the Lord, walk in Him.** There is no need to change your beliefs. Stick to what you have heard; stay the course. If you do, your life-style will be pleasing to the Lord, because you know what this Lord Jesus you received requires of you, and you can continue to mature in it, becoming more and more like Him. If you accept the new doctrines swirling round you, your life-style will also be affected—adversely. So **walk** in accordance with the Christ you **received**. Notice in this admonition the importance of truth to life. You can't separate them as some think. Truth and error will always "out." You will discover the fruit of the Spirit only in those who understand and follow the Spirit's Word.

If you want to **walk in Him** (v. 6) you must be **rooted and built up in (or by) Him**, continuing firmly in **the faith** that you were **taught** and grateful for it. If you gripe and complain, rather than allow **thanksgiving to overflow** in your heart, you will fail. Right there, you can see, many counselees run aground. They start looking around for something more satisfying, when what they really need is to be eternally grateful for what they have. Instead, they look for "something more," whereas what they need is really more of the something they already have. You can't (don't need to) add anything else to the faith of Jesus Christ. He has given you

7   having been rooted and being built up in Him, and being confirmed in the faith just as you were taught, and overflowing with thanksgiving.

8 See to it that nobody takes you captive through philosophy and empty deceit that has to do with human tradition and the worldly elements, rather than those that have to do with Christ.

---

that to which nothing else can even begin to hold a candle. What you need is to appreciate and appropriate what you have and to enter into it fully out of gratitude and thanksgiving. Many counselees need a new appreciation of what they already possess. You may have to spell that out to them in no uncertain terms (perhaps, in the sort of terms that I have just written).

Verse 8 is extremely pertinent to counseling. Here Paul warns against humanly-concocted philosophies that at bottom are empty, although they are presented to the public as substantive. Their adherents dabble in issues having to do with supposed elementary factors of life (perhaps here referring to the earth, air, fire and water theories of Greek philosophy), but they are really empty and vain. Why is this important for counselors? Because the same holds true of the 250[+] viewpoints on counseling (in America alone) that purport to have substance, but, when examined, turn out to be empty and ineffective. Claims (as here) are high but performance is low, and these systems, when carefully considered, are found not only to have nothing **to do with Christ**, but, in fact, teach theological viewpoints contrary to the Bible.

Freud, Rogers, Skinner and the rest actually were theologians (I did not say *good* ones). They taught doctrines about man, God and the universe. All thought that you could bring about love, joy, peace, etc., apart from the gospel and the Spirit, whereas, in Galatians 5 it is plain that these qualities are the **fruit of the Spirit**. Their theologies conflict with the Bible. Freud taught that man is not responsible for what he does, whereas the Scriptures teach that after death, God will not only hold him responsible, but judge each individual. Rogers said that at the core of his being man is essentially good and, therefore, should look nowhere else than within for the answers to his problems; all authorities were to be abandoned. The Bible teaches man is essentially evil and that answers and the help needed to access them must come from the outside. Absolute conflict of diametrically-opposed views, again. Skinner taught that man is nothing more than an animal and must be trained like one. The Bible teaches man's unique creation, above animals; once more there is a sheer conflict

9   In Him all the fullness of deity dwells bodily,
10   and you too are filled in Him Who is the Head of all rule and authority,

---

of views. When seen as referring to theological doctrines in conflict with the Bible, it is clear how Paul's warning in verse 8 is highly pertinent.

The interesting thing is that Paul speaks of being **taken captive** by the proponents of these views. That is an apt picture of what is done today by the self-styled professionals in the counseling field. They exercise every sort of pressure to enlist (or capture, if you will) every worker in the area—including preachers. It takes willingness to resist, to be slandered, to be misrepresented and to be attacked to withstand the wholesale propaganda and pressure tactics they employ. It is the respectable thing to be **taken captive**! Do you want to be a respectable slave or a despised freeman?

The focus of counseling must not be on psychology, but, instead, on Jesus Christ, Who (Paul observes) is indwelt by the fullness of God in His body. It is not as if God was only with or on Christ; He was *within* Him in absolute fullness. And, because you are in union with Him, there is available to you all that that fullness means. He is the Head of all rule and authority within the Church and without. What more could you want? That is the point that Paul is making—you have all you could ever need in Christ. Why turn elsewhere? The same point could be made with reference to effecting change through biblical counseling (cf. II Timothy 3:17).

Perhaps it is because of the pressures that are exerted on biblical counselors that, sometimes, they tend to offer the counselee little expectation of change. Perhaps it is because they, themselves, only half believe God's promises! But, whatever the reason, it seems that many are reluctant to speak with the authority and hope that is apparent in the words we are now examining. It is high time for counselors who claim to believe the Bible to offer what only they can: the fact that Jesus Christ can deal *definitively* with any and all problems occasioned by sin. There is neither need nor excuse to promise anything less, let alone turn elsewhere for the source of power and change.

Now, being reckoned to have lived the righteous life of Christ from the outset through to the resurrection, in which He fulfilled every requirement of the law perfectly, it is true that every believer is counted to be circumcised in Christ. This is not a physical circumcision (it **wasn't done by hand**), it is true; it is a circumcision of the heart. But while physical circumcision meant membership in the covenant people, it was always nec-

11 in Whom also you were circumcised (with a circumcision that wasn't done by hand) by the putting off of the body of flesh in Christ's circumcision,

12 being buried together with Him in baptism, in which you were raised together with Him through faith by the working of God Who raised Him from the dead.

---

essary to have the inward circumcision of the heart for membership in the spiritual body of those who were saved (cf. Dt. 19:16; 30:6; Jer. 4:4; 6:10; 9:26; Ezk. 44:7). In the end it is spiritual circumcision that counts.

Circumcision symbolized the putting off of the old person (the body of flesh = the body wrongly habituated by one's sinful nature; cf. Romans 2:28,29; 4:9-12). Today, as Paul indicates in verse 12, Spirit baptism has exactly the same import. His readers need not be physically circumcised; they have been baptized by the Spirit into Christ, i.e., into His entire experience including His circumcision, death, burial, resurrection, ascension and seating in the heavenlies (N.B., Paul does not say they were baptized into *water*, but into *Christ*). By faith they are reckoned to have accomplished all this themselves (v. 12).

Counselees that are caught up in outward rites and ceremonies of life make the mistake against which Paul wishes to guard them by these words. If they are in Christ, they have it all. Ceremonies have their place, but being in Christ is the all-important fact. That is the import of verse 13. While dead in trespasses and sins, they were unsaved gentiles who had no place, even in the outward covenant community, not being physically circumcised. But now, they are spiritually alive by faith, forgiven of all their sins. The handwritten claim against them (the debt of an unfulfilled law) has been removed; God nailed it to the cross by nailing His Son who paid off the debt by His death. By that cross, He disarmed the enemy—took away the one thing he could use to fight against us—all the while publicly exposing his evil intentions and triumphing over him in it. All this is the result of the cross. Many counselees act as if the enemy were still in possession of their souls (and there are counselors who do the same). No, Jesus Christ has triumphed over the enemy. He no longer holds authority or power over counselees Counselors and counselees alike must think and act in accordance with the fact that the enemy of their souls, while still kicking up a fuss, is a defeated foe. Counseling, therefore, should be carried on in a hopeful manner, with great expectations from the One Who freed the counselee from the dominion of darkness and translated him into

13 You who were dead in trespasses and the uncircumcision of your flesh, He made alive together with him, forgiving you of all of your trespasses,

14 erasing the handwritten certificate of indebtedness with its requirements that stood against us. He has taken it away from us, nailing it to the cross.

---

the kingdom of light. The atmosphere ought to be one of assurance, hope and expectation. When failures come, in some cases, that may mean that the counselee lacks salvation. After other possible reasons for failure have been eliminated (see my "Fifty Failure Factors" in *The Christian Counselor's New Testament*), check for this possibility. But only then.

According to the words of the verses just considered, there is no need for any change or addition. The Colossians have everything they need to live victorious lives for Jesus Christ. Jewish Gnosticism (or was it a gnostic Judaism?) was not only wrong but utterly unnecessary. That is precisely our contention: if Scripture affords all that is necessary to change people in ways that please Christ, anything else is not only wrong but unnecessary. Paul now begins to deal with some of the particulars that have been proposed that are useless and nonproductive for the Christian who "has everything (vv.16-23)."

The first two items on his hit list are the requirements to observe the dietary laws and to keep special days. He mentions the censorious attitude of the Judaizers. Legalists, now, as then, seem always to have the same judgmental ways. It is something to look for in counselees. There is a certain sense of superiority among those who keep their list of items (which usually is added to the Bible) that makes them think that they are in a position to judge others about these matters. Their spirit is truly gnostic: "we know what you don't and are, therefore, superior."

Here it was dietary matters first of all. These Judaizers were attempting to resurrect laws that God, in a revelation to Peter, had canceled (Acts 10). They also called for the keeping of the yearly feasts, monthly new moon observances and the weekly Sabbath—all of which had their symbolism fulfilled in Christ. Some wonder about the Sabbath. Christians do not keep the Sabbath; they observe the Lord's Day, which has *replaced* the Sabbath. All of this was a throwback to the Old Testament laws and ceremonies just as circumcision was.

That these things were symbolic and done away with because the reality that they foreshadowed had come is Paul's point in verse 17. The

15 Disarming rulers and authorities, God publicly exposed them, triumphing over them in Him.

16 So then, you must allow nobody to judge you about eating and drinking or about feasts or new moons or sabbaths,

17 which are shadows of what was coming (the body belongs to Christ).

18 You must allow nobody to disqualify you from receiving your prize, delighting in humility and the worship of angels, giving all sorts of details about what he has seen in visions, being puffed up for no reason by the mind of his flesh,

---

body (the reality that casts the shadow) is Christ; and it is the body that counts, not the shadow cast by it. That is the issue to join with those who insist on bringing in Old Testament laws that were fulfilled in Him. Today, there is a tendency in some circles to do just that. It must be avoided.

Now Paul commands the reader not to **allow** anyone to disqualify himself from the prize of eternal life by worshipping another god—i.e., humbling himself before creatures rather than the Creator, or by worshipping angels. Judaistic gnosticism had progressed to the place where the true God had been replaced by myriads of angels. There seems to have been a fascination with angels among the pseudepigraphic writers (see Charlesworth's two volumes) that ultimately developed into worship of false gods. This religion, in those who adopted it, would **disqualify** them for the **prize of eternal glory**.

These heretical teachers based their claims not only on Old Testament ceremonial laws, but on doctrine supposedly received by special revelation (18). The whole concoction of ideas sounds at one moment like legalism, at another like New Age thinking today. It was clearly an eclectic mix. And, because they claimed special knowledge and observed rigorous laws, its proponents were **puffed up** with pride and superiority. Even though they had no reason to view themselves so highly, their **minds** were not Spirit-driven, but driven by passions and purposes of the **flesh** (v. 18). Their minds, and, therefore, their system, was conceived by minds that desired to serve the flesh. Their flesh *directed* their minds. All of which means that they were unconverted persons. Counselees who become entangled in such systems need to be warned, as Paul warns his readers here, about the unconverted nature of those who teach such falsehood.

It is the heresy of the system that moves them away from the Head (Jesus Christ). The warning is that these men do not hold to the truth that

19 rather than holding fast to the Head, from Whom the whole body, supplied and held together by joints and ligaments, grows with growth brought about by God.

20 If you died together with Christ to the worldly elements, why do you live as if you were still subject to the world's requirements:

21 "Don't touch, don't taste, don't handle"?

Christ is the Head of His Church, as He is of all other things (cf. Chapter One). They have lost hold on this all-important fact. Thus, if the Colossians are not careful, they too will stray from this essential truth. The whole body of God's true children takes its sustenance from the Head. Christ is the King of His Church and provides everything for it. It will grow under His headship and under it alone (cf. Ephesians 4:16). The emphasis, once more, must always be placed on Christ. Any growth in the Church will be His doing—whether or not that growth is in the entire body, a congregation or an individual. Many counselees fail to grow simply because they are trying to grow by keeping legalistic lists. And, as a result, they neglect (purposely, or otherwise) the important matters that would bring about **growth**. But when one grows it is not by legalism; rather, it is because the **Head** of the Church has blessed him by His Spirit Who has enabled him to appropriate and integrate biblical truth into life. No one, therefore, has reason to be **puffed up**. **God** is to be praised for all true growth (v. 19).

The viewpoints of the world—it's presuppositional and basic principles—should be left behind since the Christian has **died** to them. In Paul's thinking, to be dead to them is to be done with them. He should live no longer according to the beliefs and practices of the philosophers (such as those of the Epicureans, whose influence was strong in the Colossian area). They had their published codes: Don't **touch, don't taste, don't handle**, which fit quite nicely into a Greek-Jewish gnostic mix.

But, as Paul observes, these rules have no eternal value; they all pertain to this temporal world (v. 22). And these dogmas are but human injunctions and teachings. That is the fundamental issue: is any given teaching from man or from God? If it contradicts, adds to or subtracts from the apostolic word (now inscribed in the New Testament) it is of human origin and profitless. Now, Paul warns, if not careful, you could be fooled. After all, they make themselves a reputation by their self-imposed worship, humiliation and asceticism (much like the Pharisees) but—and this is the point—all of those things fail to **keep the flesh** (the body

22   These refer to things that are all intended to be used up and perish, according to human injunctions and teachings.

23   Of course, they have a reputation for wisdom because of their self-imposed worship and supposed humility, and ascetic treatment of the body, but those things are of no value in keeping the flesh from satisfying itself.

---

wrongly habituated) **from satisfying itself**. Their system does not keep one from sin. The flesh must be put off, but these humanly-devised means are all show and not substance. That is because they fail to change the human heart.

Thus it is precisely when the counselee proposes to follow some legalistic scheme, propounded by man, as the means of solving his problems of sinful behavior, that you should haul out verse 23 and read it to him loudly and clearly. It will be of no avail. All psychology is legalistic. It could not be otherwise since it rejects the grace of God in Jesus Christ. The true solution is to put off the works of the flesh by replacing them with the fruit of the Spirit. Nothing less will do.

CHAPTER 3

---

1 So then, if you were raised together with Christ, seek the things that
are above, where Christ is seated at God's right hand.

The **so then**, with which Chapter Three begins is the conclusion to
the argument begun in Chapter Two. "On the basis of what I have been
saying," Paul continues, "which is that you were **raised together with
Christ** and seated in the heavenlies with Him, you should **seek those
things that are above**, where Christ is seated in the place of power,
authority and honor—at God's right hand." To be identified with Christ by
being united with Him through Spirit baptism, means that God reckons all
that has transpired in the life of the God-man as having happened to you
as a believer. Therefore, if your status before God is that of one who has
been resurrected and raised to the right hand of God (in Christ), the interests you pursue ought to be those having to do with the heavenly kingdom.

There is too much emphasis in the modern church on present-day
life. The church in America for too long has had it too good. Perhaps the
best thing that could happen to us, short of a revival of the faith, is to be
subjected to a wave of persecution that would strip away all of the temporal props on which we lean. At any rate, it may be true of some of your
counselees that they have had to sacrifice some of these earthly supports,
through financial reverses, or whatever, and now are in desperation wondering where security may be found. With such persons you may have an
unparalleled opportunity to help them to begin to **seek those things that
are above**.

On the other hand, like Paul, you may have to challenge those whose
temporal supports are still in place to **seek** things eternal and invisible.
Usually, these things will not come to him on their own; they must be
sought. In verse two, he says the same thing in a different way with a
slightly different slant: **keep your mind on things that are above**. Once
having obeyed the command to **seek** in verse 1, it is appropriate to
remember the admonition in verse 2 that the constant orientation of the
Christian's **mind** must be on heavenly things. Does that mean that the
heavenly-minded believer is so heavenly- minded he is no earthly good,
as some have charged? No, precisely the opposite is true. Whether the
world recognizes it or not, the believer who is truly heavenly-minded is of

2   Keep your mind on things that are above, not on those things that are
on the earth;

---

more earthly value than he would be otherwise. That is because on earth
he acts in accordance with heavenly principles, as the Lord's prayer says
when it talks about God's **will being done on earth as it is in heaven**.
That means that he does those things that benefit others as well as himself
to God's glory. Nothing more important could happen to his family, to
those around him at work and to his church. In a sense, the counselor's
whole work is to encourage believers to become more and more heavenly-
minded—in the best sense of that term.

That the believer died with Christ to his former life is clear from the
previous chapter. Well, then, says Paul, if so, your spiritual life flowing
from your union with Christ is not yet apparent; it is hidden by God. People do not know that God Himself dwells in you in the Person of the Holy
Spirit. But when Christ returns, and it is manifested who is/is not of God,
your identification with Him will be made apparent. You will appear in
the glory of heaven that you will openly share. There may not be much
left here in this world for your counselee to lean on; he may have been
divested of much of his worldly goods. But there is much to look forward
to. When you enable him to look upward, you also make it possible for
him to look forward with joy and anticipation. Many counselees are back-
ward-looking in orientation. That is because they are downward looking
for answers to their problems. When you help counselees obtain an
upward orientation, looking toward God and the glories of the heavenly
existence, you will also develop in them a forward look that will abolish
the hurtful backward resentments, queries and incriminations that may be
destroying life. One can look backward in a proper fashion only when he
has first developed the upward-forward look.

Think of it—to appear with Christ in glory! Of what importance are
the difficulties, the slights, the misrepresentations, the deprivations of this
life when compared to that? To develop this attitude in your counselee is
of the utmost importance. After all, inequities and problems in this world
will never be resolved here. And if he fails to view them in the light of
eternity he will continue to be miserable, sour and resentful. The answer
to such attitudes—above all else—is to help him to **seek** and **keep** his
mind on things **above**. If you do not have an upward orientation, of
course, it will be hard for you to help your counselee develop one. But if,
like your Lord, you have learned to **endure for the joy set before you**,

3   you died, and your life has been hidden with Christ in God.
4   When Christ (Who is our life) appears, then you also will appear with Him in glory.
   5 So then, put to death the habits of the members of your earthly body—sexual immorality, uncleanness, passion, evil desire, and greed (which is idolatry).

---

you will help many.

In Christ, you have died to the old life (v. 3). That is the fact to urge counselees to keep in mind whenever tempted to return to the old ways. And, though others may not be aware of it, you are as protected in God as is the Lord Jesus Christ Himself. Some day they will become aware that you are God's child because of the grace shown you through Jesus Christ when He returns to right all wrongs. Nothing will be hidden in that day; you will appear where you were all the while (though others did not know it)—with Him. The only difference is that then you will visibly bask in the glory of God. Keeping one's focus on that day helps one to get over the inglorious things said and done to him now. Remind your counselee of that fact.

If the counselee died to the old ways, why walk in them any longer? It is now important to kill off the old habitual patterns to which the various members of his body have been habituated. Paul says put them to death (v. 5)! This body has been taught by the unredeemed, sinful nature with which you were born to desire immorality, uncleanness, passion, evil desire and idolatrous greed. The process of killing the old sinful ways is what Jesus was talking about when He told us to **take up the cross daily**. The cross was an instrument of death. He was saying "Kill those desires, wants, practices of yours that are out of accord with my Word and replace them with those things that please Me (**follow Me**)." The task is a **daily** one, as Jesus said., never completed in this life. Gradually, one by one, new patterns of life will replace old ones as your habitual responses to circumstances. Self and the Spirit are at odds; Christ must win out over self in the struggle between the two. Counselors side with the Spirit over against the self. That is one reason why it is utterly inconsistent for Christian counselors to promote the doctrines of the self-esteem movement.

Following up the exhortation of verse 5 (a powerful verse for counselees to encounter in the counseling room), Paul goes on to say that the sins listed there are not trifles (as some might have treated them). No, it is because of such things that the **wrath** of God will fall (v. 6). There are

6   It is because of these things that God's wrath is coming.

7   At one time, indeed, you walked in these things, when you lived in them,

8   but now, put away all such things—wrath, anger, malice, blasphemy, dirty talk out of your mouth.

9   Don't lie to one another, since you have put off the old person with his practices,

10   and have put on the new person who is being renewed in such a way as to produce full knowledge that is in keeping with the image of his Creator.

---

counselees who do treat sin (or at least some sins) as not really all that bad after all—or, not all that big a deal. Why they do so is unimportant; that they do is all-important. Until one has been made fully cognizant of the heinous nature of a sin in God's eyes, he is unlikely to want to do anything about it—or, at least, do very much. Verse 6 is designed to meet that very problem: Paul points out that these matters are so important that He will send wrath because of them. And, notice, **greed** is even included in the list (which, of course, is not exhaustive).

At one time, he observes, his readers **walked in these things** (v. 7). And, Paul is right on target—these are the things that characterize many in the unsaved world. **But now** they are to put them away. And he even adds a few more items to the list—lest they think that the former one is all he had in mind: verses 8 and 9. Lists like these are convenient to read to counselees, asking them to locate themselves and their behavior in them. Sometimes you will have to explain words in them. For instance, **blasphemy** doesn't only mean speaking evil things about God, but about anyone; husbands about wives and vise versa. Become familiar with them and use them frequently.

Verse 9 says that (in Christ) you are reckoned to have already put off the old person that you were, along with the practices that were part of that life. Why then exhort us to put them off (v. 8)? Because what in Christ we are reckoned to be is not what we are in reality. He is saying *become what you are*. Become in daily living what God considers you to be as He sees you clothed in Christ's righteousness. And, just as you are reckoned to have put on all the righteous ways that accord with biblical principles, so too, you must become in practice what you are in the sight of God (v. 10). It is the gradual restoration of **the image of God** in man that is taking place as one puts off the old and replaces it with the new. This image, in part, is the **renewal** of the **full knowledge** that God has given to His own. For all of the verses now being considered, see com-

11 Here there is no place for Greek and Jew, circumcision and uncircumcision, barbarian, Scythian, slave and freedman, but rather Christ is all and is in all.

---

ments made on the parallel passages in Ephesians 4.

In the church, and before God, as Christians are being sanctified, no one has the advantage over another. All, alike, are the same in God's sight; all alike have the same opportunities for growth pleasing to God (v. 11). The only One Who really counts is Christ Himself; He is all and is in all (11). When counselees complain about the advantages one has over another, remind them that while that may be true in this life, as it is now lived by sinners, it certainly is not true before God. And, be sure they hear you say in addition, that is the only advantage that really counts!

In verse 12 we reach a new conclusion: **so then**. If we are to live according to heavenly things, we must know what they are, so that we may **put them on** in place of those sinful ways that we discard. Verses 12-17 give us a wonderful list of the heavenly virtues that may become a part of our lives here and now. It is of use to take a close look at them so that you will know exactly how to use them in counseling.

Paul reminds the readers in Colossae that they are people **chosen** by God (notice, the New Testament chosen people are no longer the Jews who are Jews racially, but those who are spiritually circumcised in Christ). And, as such, they are like God Himself—**holy** (set apart) and **dear** to Him. God cares about them and how they live their lives here. Well, what should God's set apart people be like? That is the burden of the rest of the verses in the paragraph.

First, they are to **put on compassion**. This is a characteristic that was largely missing from the ideals of paganism. It was the compassion of Christ for the sick and needy that changed the way people think about such matters. Christians ought always be characterized by compassion. Yet compassion is one element that is often missing from the counseling room. People bent on getting "fair treatment" or getting even with others speak in the most uncompassionate terms. This should be pointed out to them by the counselor and they should be held to the standard of this verse. "After all, if it were not for the compassion of Christ," you may powerfully observe, "you would never have become God's dear children."

Kindness, the second item on Paul's list, is akin to compassion. Whereas compassion is the motivating factor, kindness is that compassion actively doing things for another. It is compassion in action. It does little

12 So then, as God's chosen people, holy and dear, put on compassion, kindness, humility, meekness and patience,

---

good to sympathize with another's plight, if the sympathy does not issue in acts of kindness to him. That is part of the problem with much counseling. It attempts to become understanding, etc., and then does nothing about the problems presented by counselees. Good counseling is always kindly in form and function. It meets needs—genuine ones.

Humility follows. Hardly anyone is as humble as he ought to be. And the self-esteem movement has not helped. Indeed, it has taught people to put themselves first and to declare how valuable they are to the rest of humanity. That the rest of humanity fails to respond in a manner consistent with the assertion is perplexing to those who have been caught up in the self-worth propaganda. So, they whine and complain about others instead of developing a proper biblical humility about themselves. What is the proper biblical humility that your counselee must put on? It is a humility that begins by acknowledging that one is totally unworthy of anything from God. Then, it admits that if Christ had not come, he would rightly deserve hell. Finally, it declares that salvation and everything worthwhile in one's life is the result of the work of Christ and His Spirit. It attributes no merit to itself.

Meekness is the willingness to confess that one is no better than another and that in the situation, where another had wronged him, he must deal with that person in such a way that he let's him know that he is no better, but might even need the assistance of the wrongdoer in the days to come. It is not weakness, but it exerts strength by means of moving gently into another's life—even when reprimanding him and calling him to repentance. Meekness is a caring for how one approaches another, all the while recognizing one's own proclivities to the very same sins.

Patience is the final virtue in verse 12. It means the willingness to do things by God's timetable. The patient person continues in spite of the problems that seem not to be resolved. He waits for others to learn and grow. He is not always shoving in his oar. He calls more on God for satisfaction, willing to wait for God to work, than on others to grant him what he wishes.

Closely aligned to patience is **putting up with one another**. How important for counselees to realize God expects this of them! There is much squabbling in homes and in churches that would be eliminated entirely if this were the practice of believers. Probably somewhere near 85

13 putting up with one another, and when anyone has a complaint against anyone, forgiving each other; just as the Lord forgave you, so too you must forgive.

14 Above all of these things, put on love, which binds the rest together into a whole.

---

to 90 percent of the counseling situations that you face involve failure to put up with someone. And, even where this is not the major problem, it is a complicating problem that otherwise impeded successful counseling. Ring the changes on this one!

Then, along the same lines, there is the exhortation to deal with **complaints** by confrontation that leads to **forgiveness**. I shall not develop the many forgiveness scenarios that I have treated in depth in my book, *From Forgiveness to Forgiving*. Again, the motivation is to remember Christ's forgiveness of you. Cf. Eph. 4:32.

In verse 14 Paul puts the capstone on the list by mentioning **love** which he places **above** all else. Why is it above the rest? Because, he says, **it binds the rest together into a whole**. But what does he mean by that.? That which **binds** one thing to another must touch both. It is important to recognize that love must be involved in (touch) all the other virtues mentioned. They must be done in love. Love is obedience to God's commandments whereby one gives himself to God and to others.

Notice that in verse 15 **Christ's peace** is the **umpire** that has the **final say**. Many have erroneously taken this to speak of guidance. But the passage does not refer to guidance. Paul does not teach that you can determine what to do by "having peace about a matter." The passage is talking about how to get along with other Christians. In the relationship one has with his fellow-believer, he is to seek peace as the key factor. He is to pursue it, promote it and produce it. Peace, here, is not peace in your hearts. The point is that in your hearts you must let the goal of peace with other Christians be the final arbiter of the ways you act toward them. Keeping this principle in mind, counselors will clearly opt for the peaceful solution over any other—so long as it compromises no biblical injunction. Note, peace maintains the unity of the **parts** that form **one body**.

And, as a parting virtue, Paul mentions **thankfulness**. The counselee who is grateful to God for all he is and has is rarely in trouble with others. And, in the attitude of thankfulness he is able to enter into work that will lead to biblical change with the right spirit.

The next verse has to do directly with counseling. A counselor who

15 Let Christ's peace have final say in your hearts, to which, indeed, you were called as parts of one body. And be thankful.

16 Let Christ's Word dwell in you richly, as you teach and counsel yourselves as wisely as possible, and as you sing psalms, hymns and spiritual songs with grace in your hearts toward God.

17 Whatever you do by word or deed, do everything in the Name of the Lord Jesus, giving thanks to God the Father through Him.

---

counsels well is one in whom Christ's Word **dwells richly**. What does that mean? That biblical teaching is *at home* in him. It does not come only occasionally for a visit. Rather, it has taken up its abode in him. To dwell in him means not only to dwell in his thinking as knowledge acquired but also as the motivating and directing force in his living. This is necessary for good teaching and counseling. And, it is to be a wealth of this Word that dwells in him. Unlike a preacher, who knows beforehand that about which he will speak, the counselor must be ready for anything. He must have a grasp of the whole counsel of God, know where to locate pertinent passages, what they mean and how to apply them to daily living. **Richly** is an apt description of that which is necessary.

Also, he must be able to teach and counsel **with all wisdom**. That is, as wisely as possible. Wisdom begins with the fear of the Lord. It is truth applied. But not merely truth; it is God's truth. And it is applied God's way for God's ends. Wisdom is the Book of Proverbs lived. And, Christ's Word must direct as one sings Psalms (Old Testament songs), hymns (New Testament songs), and spiritual songs (more personally oriented songs). And this happens rightly when they are sung from the heart (sincerely) as the result of God's grace at work within. That grace will direct one's teaching, counseling, singing toward God.

Then, in verse 17, a summary statement: **whatever you do...** Whether one is speaking or acting, he must do so in Christ's Name, thankfully. That about sums up the entire Christian life. You can always ask a recalcitrant counselee, "Can you do what you are contemplating in Christ's Name?" If he cannot justify his words or actions thusly, you must call on him to refrain. And, it is of importance to do and say those things that can be justified in a thankful spirit. Otherwise, one's best efforts can be ruined by his foul manner. Note, in passing, that all prayer—even thanksgiving—must be in Christ (through Him). People who attempt to get a hearing with God in their own Names are sadly mistaken to think that God will receive them. All we have that is good, or ever will have, comes through Him.

18 Wives, submit yourselves to your husbands, as is fitting in the Lord.

19 Husbands, love your wives and don't be bitter toward them.

20 Children, obey your parents about everything, since this pleases the Lord.

21 Fathers, don't irritate your children, or they may become exasperated.

Now, throughout the rest of the chapter, in brief, Paul takes up those authority/submission relationships that he develops at length in the Book of Ephesians. See comments there. In this place, I wish only to mention those additional comments that more fully enhance the understanding of a relationship as Ephesians is amplified by Colossians. The statement in verse 18, **it is fitting** is one of those. It adds additional insight into Paul's thinking. Not only is it right, because of the authority of the husband, but to the community in which Christians live it bears a witness—it is the fitting thing. Doubtless, there will be times in which that motivation should be uppermost in your counseling advice. Keep it in mind. Certain things are done (or not done) because those who are **in the Lord** know that such behavior is **fitting**.

Husbands are not only to love their wives, but the additional thought of not having a **bitter** attitude toward them is presented. Perhaps bitterness has led to as much heartache in marriage as any other. Husbands must deal with their problems daily, not allowing them to pile up, harden, and crystallize into bitterness. Always check for bitterness and resentment in husbands who are failing to exert Christian leadership.

Children are to obey parents **since this pleases the Lord**. That motivation is higher than the one mentioned in Ephesians (that things will go well and they will live long on the land). In Ephesians Paul does also mention that it is right to do so. But, here, the highest, warmest motivation is given—to please the Lord. Every child ought to progress from personal gain, or mere duty, to doing things to please the Lord. There is a progression in motivation inherent in these items. All are proper motivations, but all are not as mature.

Fathers are not to irritate children so that they throw up their hands in exasperation (v. 21). Counselees having problems with children often fail to heed this command. They nag, change the rules, are inconsistent in punishing and, in a dozen other ways, irritate children who eventually, out of exasperation, give up. The children shouldn't; but the parents shouldn't put the temptation in their way. Fathers, who are mentioned in both books,

22 Slaves, obey your earthly lords about everything, not only when they are watching you work, as people-pleasers do, but rather, with singleness of heart, fearing the Lord.

23 Whatever you do, work at it heartily for the Lord and not for men,

24 knowing that from the Lord you will receive an inheritance as a reward. Christ is the Lord for Whom you work as a slave!

25 Now the one who does wrong will receive what he deserves for his wrongdoing, and there must be no partiality.

---

are responsible to see that these commands are fulfilled.

More is now said about **slaves** than anything else. Perhaps because the institution caused so much trouble. The phrase, **with singleness of heart**, is a slight twist on the words in Ephesians. One ought to obey and serve sincerely, not out of mixed motives. Moreover, he is to do it **heartily—for the Lord**. He works for Christ even as a slave, and it is Christ, therefore, who will give him the reward.

Verse 25 probably refers to the master, not to the slaves. They are to treat all fairly. And, if they mistreat their slaves, they too will be subject to discipline for their wrongdoing. In Chapter Four you will learn more about slave masters, since the chapter division cuts right through the middle of Paul's discussion.

Doubtless this will become a favorite chapter of many counselors. It is chocked full of useful helps for counseling people in almost any sort of situation. Learn it thoroughly, use it frequently and you will become a successful counselor.

CHAPTER 4

1 Lords, treat your slaves with justice and fairness, knowing that you also have a Lord in heaven.
2 Persevere in prayer, being alert in it with thanksgiving,
3 praying at the same time also about us, that God may open for us a door for the Word, to speak about the secret of Christ, because of which I am in bonds,
4 so that I may proclaim it clearly, as I ought to.

Chapter Four is a continuation of the material on slaves and masters that was introduced in the previous chapter and makes an unfortunate break in the continuity of the material. The slave is to be treated by the Christian Lord with **justice and fairness**—probably the elements that were most neglected by those who held absolute sway over others. Therefore, following these injunctions would become a witness in the community as well as a benefit to the slave and ultimately do away with slavery altogether. The Lord of the Christian slave master gave these instructions to him, reminding him that he too is a slave of such a Master as He desires him to become. Christian businessmen have for far too long adopted the ways of the world. Instead, they should take these words to heart as they contemplate directing their employees. And employees must work for their employers just as the previous injunctions directed slaves to do. Job counseling should depend heavily on the concluding words of Chapter Three.

Verses 3 and 4 contain a request for prayer, similar to, but different from, the request found in the final chapter of Ephesians. Here too, he wants the reader to pray regularly, alert to items of significance and with thanksgiving for answers. But in those prayers uttered on Paul's behalf he wants them to pray not only for opportunities to preach the Word, but also that he may preach it as **clearly** as he ought to. Many counselees complain about their pastors' preaching. And, in particular, about the confusing, fuzzy ways in which they preach. Ask them: "How often do you pray for your pastor to preach clearly?" It is the duty and privilege of every believer to do so. If Paul needed prayer for his preaching, don't you think your pastor does too?

Paul wanted to make known the mystery about Christ. That too must be your desire and objective in all counseling. Keep the death and resurrection of Jesus Christ before your counselees at all times. No matter what

5 Walk in wisdom before those who are outside, making the most of opportunities.

---

their problems, it is how the gospel affects them that counts. You also need the prayers of your counselees so that you will be able to counsel them with clarity and insight.

But, having said that Paul, thinking of his own speech (like him, the counselor must at all times be aware of and work on his), extrapolates to the speech of his readers (vv. 5,6). He begins by admonishing them to **walk in wisdom before those who are outsiders** (unbelievers). This **wisdom** is the practical use of biblical truth and principles (see above on 3:16) in relationship to the lost. How Christians act (but, especially, how they talk) is one of the ways that God uses to attract unbelievers to the gospel. It is often true that the problem your counselee has is with unbelievers (those who are **outside** the church). You must be able to help him to see how to handle relationships with those outside. How one handles his relationships in such contexts can be crucial to a good witness for Jesus Christ.

Not only should he look for **opportunities** to speak about Christ and **make the most of** them ("Let me tell you how I found an answer to that problem when I faced it"), but he should take every strained relationship with unbelievers (the kind you hear about in counseling all the time) as an opportunity to witness. All you need to do is to retrace the vices to avoid and the virtues to follow that are listed toward the end of the previous chapter of Colossians and apply them to the situation at hand. In following the Lord's Word in those regards one makes opportunities out of seemingly difficult circumstances. An in-depth relationship with another, even though he is an unbeliever and even though it is a strained one, is the sort of opportunity you want your counselee to make the most of. Most other relationships with unbelievers are too superficial to be able to utilize as a witnessing context. But, when he sees your counselee handling a difficult situation **wisely**, he is more than likely to be impressed.

But, again, as James makes clear, it is in our speech (with unbelievers as well as with Christians) that we are most likely to trip on our own shoe laces and defeat our best intentions. That is why Paul focuses on speech in these several verses—the gospel is a *message* and must be expressed verbally. Therefore, it is essential to honor Christ through speech. In verse 6 Paul reveals the true method for learning to speak to unbelievers well: **Let your speech at all times be gracious, seasoned with salt.** What he is

6   Let your speech at all times be gracious, seasoned with salt, so that you may know how to answer everyone.

---

saying is, "Don't be careful how you speak just when a problem with an unbeliever arises; rather, be careful about (and work on) how to speak properly *in all circumstances at all times*. Then you will know how to speak when in the clutch." That means that he should be concerned to honor Christ in his speech around the home with his wife and children, at church with other believers, etc. If, in those easier situations he learns how to be **gracious, seasoning his speech with salt** (making it pleasant— appetizing), he will automatically, unconsciously, smoothly and skillfully say the right things when talking to unbelievers. These four traits, so desirable in this sort of context, are the characteristics of habit. Habits are best learned by daily effort in nonthreatening circumstances. Then, under pressure, they come to the fore as faithful servants. Habits of gracious speech are best developed by daily effort in ordinary circumstances. Impress these facts on counselees.

Under the pressure of **answering** the unbeliever (and the believer alike; note well Paul's **everyone**) you will must know how to speak wisely. Paul is interested in how we speak to unbelievers, but by his use of **everyone** in verse 6, indicates that God wants us to use gracious speech in addressing believers as well. Think of how much controversy at home and in the church could be avoided by the effort of all to learn to speak **wisely and graciously**. Well, you may not be able to reach all, but those counselees who are under your care should know that God requires gracious speech of them at all times, with **everyone**. One way in which you may emphasize this fact is by not allowing counselees to use anything other than **gracious** speech in the counseling session. And, of course, as a counselor, you must set the example of such speech. When listening to a counselee address another (perhaps a husband is speaking to his wife) in such derogatory and nasty language, I have found myself from time to time having to say something like, "You are not going to talk that way to one another *here*. Such hateful language is obviously one of the reasons why you are here. But you are not going to be here very long unless you make an effort to speak as Christians should. There may not be much gracious language spoken between you, but this is the one hour during the week, at least, when there will be nothing less. 'Now, Jim, let's try saying that again to Mary; only this time in a way that would honor the Lord and help her.'"

7 Tychicus, our dear brother and faithful servant and fellow slave in the Lord, will give you all the facts about me.

8 I sent him to you for this very purpose, so that you may know all about us and that he may encourage your hearts.

9 Onesimus, our faithful and dear brother (who is one of you), is coming along with him; they will tell you everything that has happened here.

10 Aristarchus, my fellow prisoner, greets you, and Mark, Barnabas' cousin (about whom you have received instructions—if he comes to you, welcome him),

---

For the rest of the chapter, Paul speaks to and about persons with whom he has worked in various ways. We shall peruse these casually, noting a few points that may be pertinent to our purposes. Tychicus is styled **a dear brother and faithful servant and fellow slave in the Lord**. There is no reason to comment on the very familiar terms Paul uses. But, the fact that he uses them, is significant. Paul was not one to flatter others. Yet was not slow to acknowledge faithfulness. Here is evidence of the fact. Counselors may tend to shy away from commending their counselees when it is proper to do so. One important thing is to give honor to whom honor is due. If someone has worked hard, acknowledge it. It will not hurt anyone to do so, but it may do a lot of good by encouraging the counselee. Tychicus was to carry all the information concerning Paul's imprisonment, how his cause was going and the likelihood of his release, when he arrived with this epistle at Colossae. Such material, Paul thought, was best conveyed by word of mouth.

He would also bring good **news** and a slant on the not-so-good news that would be encouraging to the readers (v. 8). To put the biblical (that is, encouraging) face on bad news as well as spread the obviously good news is an important function of Christ's faithful servants. Counselors are to become biblically valid spin doctors! After all, those with God's viewpoint are the only ones who can honestly become such.

Again, there are good words for **Onesimus**. Turn to the Book of Philemon to learn about him. **Aristarchus**, who was in prison with Paul, sends greetings too. Paul worked with a team; rarely did things alone. Here we get a glimpse of how others were suffering for Christ as well as he.

There are words about **Mark,** who now seems to be in Paul's favor once more after the parting of the ways some years before. Yet, there is something that must be done with reference to him (perhaps, help that he needs in the process of restoring him to the gospel ministry) instructions

11 and Jesus who is called Justus. These men are my only co-workers for God's empire from the circumcision, and they have proved to be an encouragement to me.

12 Epaphras, who is one of you and a slave of Christ Jesus, greets you. He is always struggling in his prayers for you, that you may stand, complete and completely certain in all of God's will.

13 I want to testify about him, that he has had much distress over you and those in Laodicea, and those in Hierapolis.

---

that Paul had previously sent. But, since there may have been questions about Mark's suitability due to the past problem with him, Paul insists that they should **welcome** him. Restoring people is important in the work of counseling—even restoring those to the ministry who, in one way or another, have failed (cf. Gal. 6:1). Here, we see Paul hard at work doing so. Never hesitate to help Christian workers regain ministerial positions when it is biblically appropriate to do so.

And, he includes **Justus**, who probably changed his name from **Jesus** out of respect for the Lord—or, at least, to avoid any confusion when speaking about himself. Paul rightly includes all these men as his co-workers for the promotion of God's empire who were converted Jews. They encouraged him constantly. The ministry of **encouragement** is a vital one. Paul needed it just as we all do. A counselor must consider the giving of encouragement a fundamental task of his. People who are discouraged will not make the efforts to change that are necessary. How does one encourage another? Not by trying to "buck him up." But by presenting the biblical viewpoint on every situation. Seeing things from God's perspective is always encouraging.

Now, he turns to gentile workers. **Epaphras**, a Colossian, sends greetings from Rome (presumably, he could not return with Tychicus). Paul lets them know that Epaphras had not forgotten them, but, rather, prayed earnestly for them on a regular basis. His concern? The same as Paul's. That they would **stand**, unmoved by those proclaiming error. He wanted them to recognize that they are **complete** in Christ, and to be **completely certain of God's will**. He, Paul informs them, has had much distress over the false teaching at Colossae and (as it seems to have spread) also in Laodicea and Hieropolis—places not too far removed. By these words they would know he was still with Paul, and that he was aware of the trouble the errorists were causing in the infant churches. Thus, the very fact that he was not ignorant of the false doctrine, but, in full understanding, rejected it, would be an additional encouragement for the read-

14 Luke, the dear physician, greets you, and Demas.

15 Greet the brothers in Laodicea, and Nympha and the church at her house.

16 When this letter has been read before you, see to it that it is read also in the Laodicean church, and that you read the one from Laodicea.

17 And tell Archippus: "Be sure that you carry out to the full the work of service that you received in the Lord."

18 The greeting is in my (Paul's) own handwriting. Remember my bonds.

May help be yours.

---

ers to resist the inroads of this false teaching.

Luke and Demas (who would later defect), greet them. Warm words are written concerning Luke. Nothing is said of Demas (was there already suspicion of him?). The Colossian church was in close fellowship with the one at Laodicea. So, there was to be a greeting to that church through them (v. 15) as well as a swapping of epistles (this one and one Paul sent to Laodicea, that has been lost). **Nympha**, who, presumably, lived in some outlying area, had a smaller congregation meeting in her house. Even that little group was not to be forgotten!

Archippus was to be encouraged by all to **carry out the full work of ministry to which the Lord called him**. Part of that work would be to protect the flock from error. Perhaps it was lack of diligence on his part in this area of ministry that allowed the errorists to get a toehold in the Colossian congregation. At any rate, the ministry of the Word is broad, pertaining to all life and godliness. And you, as a Christian counselor, must not neglect any aspect of it. Perhaps, as much as anything else, the study of this letter (like the study of the rest) makes the far-ranging territory of biblical ministry a reality.

Closing words: This letter is from me, Paul (look at the conclusion written in the distinctive letters of my own handwriting). It is not easy suffering for Christ; please do not forget my bonds. Pray for me. Send whatever help you can. Those are the thoughts compacted into that last, terse statement. The words acknowledge a genuine need; but they are neither whining words not pathetic ones. They are the honest words of a steadfast soldier of Christ.

Introduction to
PHILEMON

This small epistle, like the other brief letters of Jude and John, was written to meet an emergency. Evidently, Paul took a piece of papyrus and hurriedly dashed off this little gem that gives us so much insight into the workings of the apostle's mind and the tact he exhibited in his ways with men. It is an inconspicuous, but valuable piece of divine revelation, without which the counselor, to say nothing of the preacher and theologian, would be seriously impoverished. We shall, therefore, try to give it all the attention that it deserves.

This prison epistle finds Paul in Rome awaiting trial by Nero. While he might have been wrapped up in his own affairs and hardly in a mood to help others—as so many of us might be under similar circumstances—instead, we discover him concerning himself with the welfare of a runaway slave and his relationship to his master. Immediately, this tells you something of the great heart of the apostle. It was truly a pastor's heart. He cares about people in the church and what he can do to further good relations between them. From this expression of deep concern, every counselor may learn much.

When you are tired, done in, about to turn in for the day and the phone rings, pastor, how do you respond? Do you groan and hope that it is not a new problem with some member of your church? I confess that all too often that is what I do. And, yet, to deal with these problems is precisely why God has placed you in that church. You ought to rejoice that He has entrusted you to bless yet another person by ministering His Word. That is a great privilege for us sinners. We deserve nothing but wrath; yet God has put into our hands the ministry of reconciliation. What grace! So, together with me, let's try to look upon each phone call as an opportunity, not only to assist another one of God's children in counseling, but, in doing so, also to express our gratitude to God for putting us into His service. It must have been something like this that motivated the heart of Paul, laden down with his own concerns, to reach out to others in need. Until you are in prison, counselor, let's not hear any of the sort of talk you know you sometimes engage in ("Why can't they solve their own problems?" "Of all times for something like this to happen!" etc.). In the sovereignty of God, providentially exercised, you are called on to minister rather than be ministered to. But, as you will see later on in the discussion of this letter, when you minister, God often provides through that very ministry a ministry to you in return.

The Epistle of Paul to
PHILEMON

1 Paul, a prisoner of Christ Jesus, and our brother Timothy to our dear friend and co-worker Philemon,

---

In verse one, as well as verse 23 of this brief letter, Paul refers to his imprisonment. Clearly, it was on his mind. Conditions were not optimal. Prisons in those days offered little or nothing for their inhabitants. Friends or family had to provide sustenance, clothing, etc. Moreover, of greater import to Paul, he would soon stand trial before Nero to answer trumped up charges against him. In that hour, as he indicates in Philippians 1, he wanted to be sure that he presented the Christian faith in a favorable light. It was the opportunity of a lifetime: to preach Christ to the emperor of the Roman empire! He wanted to go face that experience in such a way that Christ was honored and the gospel was proclaimed That was his principal concern.

Yet, with that facing him, and in the squalor and stench of a Roman cell, he is thinking of others. But, he would not miss the opportunity to make the point that he is in prison *not* because the Jews had accused him or because the Romans had locked him up, but because Jesus wanted him there: he was a **prisoner of Christ Jesus**. This, too, was a part of his ministry. Paul includes Timothy as a co-writer of this letter to Philemon. He calls Timothy "our brother." The language of the New Testament is revealing. Paul rightly thought of the entire Church of Christ as a great family—the family of God. It was his task, among others, to promote brotherly love among the members of that family. So, even the very terms that he uses (to say nothing of the frequent references to individual Christians in this and other letters) are calculated to emphasize that point. Counselors are involved in the use of language to change people in ways that please God. They should be extremely careful, therefore, about the words that they use. Not only ought they to abandon the psychological jargon that is so very unhelpful, misleading and non-communicative and replace it with biblical words that accurately describe human conditions, but like Paul, they also should choose to use language in everyday writing and speaking that builds up individual Christians and the congregations to which they belong. Timothy *was* a brother in Christ; it was important, therefore, to remind Philemon of the fact.

2   and to Apphia our sister, and Archippus our fellow soldier and to the church at your house:

And, again, by emphasizing the brotherhood of all those whom God has called, Paul was laying groundwork for what he wanted to request of Philemon—the forgiveness and manumission of Onesimus. This great family of faith consisted of brothers and sisters. Philemon needed to be (subtlety) reminded of the fact. As we shall see, it will not be long before Paul will be referring to Onesimus, himself, as a "brother" (v. 16).

Who was **Philemon**? A convert of the apostle Paul (cf. v. 19). He was known for his hospitality (an important matter in those days): verses 5-7. And, Paul considered him a co-worker (v. 1). That the church at Colossae met in his home (v. 2) and that he owned slaves, indicates that he was probably a man of means.

At any rate, Paul had remained close to him, and in this letter, evidences a warm and convivial spirit when writing. **Apphia**, in accordance with the Paul's interest in stressing the brotherhood of all true believers, is called a **sister**. On the other hand, **Archippus** is styled a **fellow-soldier**. Presumably, he had been through several spiritual battles fighting alongside of Paul. The traditional view is that Archippus was the son of Philemon and Apphia. While we cannot be sure of this, the order of names, and the position of the information concerning the house church, lend some credence to this view. However, Colossians 4:17 seems to indicate that he was (also?) pastor of the congregation.

Note a fact that is often missed in dealing with this letter: it is not written to Philemon alone. Archippus, Apphia and the entire congregation are addressed as fellow-recipients of the letter. Why is that? Presumably, because Paul had something difficult to request of Philemon, he was enlisting everyone around him, who had influence on him, to help him to make the right decision. A counselor will be wise to do the same. Often precisely what counselees need to proceed with their homework during periods between counseling sessions is the encouragement of others who may be enlisted to help. That point must not be lost in noting the recipients of the letter.

Paul wishes them **help** (the second meaning of grace) and **peace** from God the Father (notice, here again, the family of faith is alluded to) **and the Lord** (that is, the One who called Paul and directs him in His service) **Jesus Christ**. These two qualities are devoutly desired by the apostle. Again and again he refers to them in various letters. Why? Because

3 May help and peace from God our Father and from the Lord Jesus Christ be yours.

---

one (peace) was the Hebrew greeting and the other (grace) the Greek salutation? No, though Paul may have adopted his greetings from those facts. For all the apostles the greetings that they give and the benedictions that they express have meaning. They are not simply epistolary formalities. All sinners need precisely these two things from God: help and peace. And, it is sure that is exactly what every counselee needs.

Counselees may take heart over the fact that, according to the apostle, these two things may be obtained from God. His wish for Philemon and his family was not in vain. Philemon would need to take a calm attitude toward what Paul was writing and make a decision in which he would have to be helped by God. Whatever the problem{s} your counselee may have, remember, he may obtain help and peace from God. There is hope in the fact. Like Paul, who makes a point of it, tell him so!

The first three verses constitute the words of greeting. But, as you have seen, they are not throwaway sentences. They have meaning; they set the tone, lay out the background and imply things to come. That Paul would spend three verses out of a meager 25 in such activity shows the importance of approaching an issue carefully by *preparing* the counselee for what is to come. Perhaps failure to so prepare for future activity in counseling sessions, in which (like Philemon) the counselee must make changes that may be inconvenient, or even costly, accounts for the resistance that is sometimes encountered when you finally get down to the nitty-gritty. Gaining commitment early on in the sessions is crucial. And while Paul is more subtle than actually asking for commitment as such, nevertheless, by all he writes he is drawing Philemon into his net.

Following the words of greeting comes the thanksgiving. Four more verses before he gets down to the issue at hand! Together with the three verses devoted to the salutation, these four make a total of *seven preparatory verses!* That is nearly one-third of the total number of verses in the letter! How important it is to prepare people for hard decisions they are likely to be called to make is clear from Paul's great care in doing so. No wonder Paul was concerned to enlist others as well. Counselor, learn from this!

Let's look at those four verses. Paul says that he **always thanks God** for Philemon **whenever he has occasion to mention him in his prayers**. That he prayed for those with whom he worked is implicit in the verse.

4 I always thank my God whenever I mention you in my prayers,
5 because I hear of your love and faithfulness that you show toward the
Lord Jesus and toward all the saints,

Prayer for counselees may also be inferred. But note, it is not the problems in Philemon's life for which Paul prayed, but, in his prayers for him he was *thankful*. When we pray for counselees, perhaps we concentrate too much on the problems they are having. That we should pray for these goes without saying, but not exclusively. The tendency, of course, is to focus on difficulties, since that is often the concern of the counseling itself. But two things may be said in this regard. First, biblical counseling should never focus on the negative. Naturally, you must deal with the problems that are presented, *but always in light of how God has an answer to them—an answer you are anxious to apply to the case at hand as soon as possible*. Secondly, that emphasis will lead to prayers of thanksgiving for all of the positive results that are apparent from the beginning of the sessions, no matter how slight they may seem. And, in addition, such thinking and praying will lead to encouraging comments such at those found in these four verses, when talking to your counselee.

For what is Paul thankful? He thinks of Philemon's **love and faithfulness toward the Lord Jesus**. Since biblical counseling is carried on only with those who know Christ as Savior (you can't get an unbeliever to change in ways that please God; cf. Romans 8:8), your counselee's faith in Christ is always one thing that you can be thankful for. Without it, there would be no hope for you to effect any significant change in him. With it, all change that God requires is possible! Now, unlike Philemon, the counselee before you at the moment may not have been so faithful to Christ and he may not have been demonstrating much love either. However, you can thank God, and tell him that you do, for the hope that comes from knowing he is one in whom the Spirit dwells and, therefore, one who has all the potential for change that God requires. And, in the course of counseling, when you begin to see change through the ministry of the Word, in the power of the Spirit, let him know of your gratitude to God for that too.

Again, note that while Philemon is commended for all he has done, Paul puts the emphasis on the fact that God is the One who has effected this in him: he does not thank Philemon, but God for these good things. In counseling, likewise, always explicitly attribute the good changes that you see to God, not to the counselee, even though *by God's grace he has worked hard to achieve it*. Ultimately, all change for good is the work of

6   praying that this sharing of your faith may have the effect of bringing
about a full knowledge of all the good things that we have in Christ.

God's Spirit (cf. Philippians 2:13). Counselees, like Paul, should be
taught to be **thankful** for all progress; not **proud** of it.

Paul is also thankful that God has put it into the heart of Philemon to
show love and faithfulness toward **all the saints**. In those days when
Christians traveled—especially those who were on missionary journeys—
it was necessary to find homes in which one could stop over on the way.
Presumably, Philemon's home had been open to them. It was also the custom to "send one forward on his journey" a semi-technical phrase among
Christians that meant to provide all the funds, food (or whatever else was
necessary) to sustain one as he traveled to the next stopover in a believer's
home. For more on this see the discussion of the point in the commentary
on II & III John.

Next, Paul says he prays that this **sharing of his faith** (i.e., the sharing with other believers the benefits of his Christian Faith) may reveal to
him and to others a **full knowledge** of all the good things that Christ has
provided for His people. As Philemon gave of his money, care and concern to others, he (and they) came to see how much Christ has made available to them—joy, fellowship, satisfaction, purpose in life, the solution to
problems, the hope of eternal life, etc. As you work with counselees, that
ought also to be your prayer for them and for those with whom they must
deal. Many counselees come thinking that there is very little to the Christian faith; they may even doubt whether it is worth continuing in it. But
that is because they center their thinking on themselves, what they lack
and wrongs that have been done to them. One of the things that you will
find necessary, as soon as it is feasible to do so, is to lead counselees into
concern for others. Only then can they and those around them appreciate
all that there is in Christ Jesus. It is more blessed to give than to receive!

Of course, one of the ways in which Philemon and those around him
could more fully appreciate the good things they have in Christ would be
for him to release Onesimus from his obligations and free him from slavery. Paul, once more is plowing the ground and readying it for the planting
of that seed.

Paul says that he is bold to hint such things because he knows *personally* the love and faithfulness of Philemon. He has experienced it. He
has known the happiness of working with him, of spending time in his
home and of seeing how he encouraged (**refreshed**) the hearts of other

7   I say this because I have enjoyed much happiness and encouragement from your love because you have revived the hearts of the saints, brother.

8 So then, although I am quite free in Christ to order you to do the proper thing,

---

believers. Then, he slips in the (already) much-used term "brother." He wants, again, to emphasize the family relationship Philemon bears to all Christians, including Onesimus. The word "brother" (and "sister") carries very strong connotations as well as denotations. It is often useful to call your counselee brother or sister when emphasizing the need for fellowship with others with whom he or she may be at odds. And, in addition, to call those others by the same name.

In verses 8-11, having laid the groundwork, Paul now confronts Philemon about the issue at hand. As he says, he has apostolic authority to **order** Philemon to do as he wishes, but he will not use that authority (cf. vv. 8, 10). This is an important point. There are times to use authority (God has granted authority to the elders of the church: cf. Hebrews 13:17), but there are times not to do so. This was one of them. How did Paul decide which way to go? As he says in verses 4-7, he knows his man. He has seen the goodness God has wrought in the heart of Philemon in relation to many others and to himself, and he was convinced, therefore, that he would free Onesimus on appeal. It is always better for a counselee to do something on his own, as the result of an appeal rather than an order, if that is possible. It strengthens the counselee to make the decision and to take the action on his own. Paul's appeal is strong and he has prepared Philemon for it, however. He does not simply bring it out of the blue.

First, notice that Paul refers to releasing Onesimus as the **proper thing**. He had no doubt that this was what God Himself wanted. That is why it was "proper." Paul was not talking about something that seemed right to society or to himself alone. When you appeal to a counselee, be sure that you, too, can refer to the contemplated action as the **biblically** proper thing. The authority of God, vested in His Word, is what you want the counselee to bow before. The authority of the servants of God only comes into play when the Word is ignored. One of your main purposes is to bring the counselee into willing subjection to the Scriptures in a very practical way.

But Paul does not hesitate also to add his own personal appeal—and an emotional one at that. Out of his **love** for Philemon, he appeals rather than orders. And, it is not just anyone asking for this favor, it is **Paul, an**

9   because of love I prefer to appeal to you—as Paul, an old man, and now also a prisoner of Christ Jesus—

10   I appeal to you for my child Onesimus to whom I have given birth in my bonds,

---

old man and now **a prisoner** to boot! Those are appeals that are not only strong, but very difficult to reject. Paul is not reluctant to draw on his personal relationship to Philemon as a basis for granting his request. May a counselor do the same? You'd better believe it! If there is any personal factor that legitimately may be added to the biblical injunction, it is not wrong to use it.

What is his appeal? It is not fully stated even at this point. It has to do with Onesimus (v. 10). That much he makes clear. But not just with Onesimus—with a new Onesimus. An Onesimus that has now, under Paul's ministry, come to faith in Jesus Christ. He calls him "my child...to whom I have given birth in my bonds." That is to say, when Onesimus ran away, he went to Rome. There for some reason or other—perhaps he was desperate for help—he looked up Paul in prison. Paul surely was well-known to him, because he had been a guest in Philemon's house many times. Perhaps Paul had even taken time on those occasions to witness to Onesimus. At any rate, when in need, he turned to Paul. And their contact in prison led to Onesimus' spiritual birth. Paul thinks of him as his spiritual child. Not everyone does, of course, but frequently, counselees—or others who know of your efforts in helping them—will come to you in time of need. Contacts made today, may not pay off for years. So, it is always important to treat everyone as if you had to deal with him for the rest of your life.

Often it is in time of need that unbelievers will come for counseling. Although it is not possible to achieve change that is pleasing to God until the unbeliever comes to faith in Christ, it is a good time to present the gospel to him and urge him to believe. Honestly tell him that God has the solution to every problem he is facing, but that these solutions cannot be accessed until he becomes a Christian. One word: warn him that he cannot pretend to become a Christian to gain access to God's solutions. Any profession of faith in Christ must be real. God looks on the hearts. A counselee may fool you for a time, perhaps, but he can't fool God. God's solutions are for God's people. He must be genuine. If, and when he is, counseling may proceed. Otherwise, you will remain in a precounseling (evangelism) mode.

11 who once was useless to you but now has become useful both to you and to me.

12 I am sending him back to you, though in doing so I send my very heart.

This new Onesimus, Paul says, is **useful**. Obviously, Paul is making a play on the name Onesimus, which means "Useful." Before, a thieving runaway, he has now become a Christian, and along with his conversion, a newly useful person, one Paul claims is useful to both Philemon and himself. Note how Paul includes himself in the statement as a first hint of what he is about to ask—not only Onesimus' freedom, but his continued service to Paul.

In verses 12-14, the full request finally comes forth. Paul has, laboriously, worked up to this climactic point. With such exquisite preparation, what can Philemon do but accede to his request? First, Paul is careful to follow the lawful requirement with regard to Onesimus: he is sending him back (v. 12) Paul is no wide-eyed, radical abolitionist. While it is his desire to see Onesimus freed, and probably, while he detests slavery as an institution, nevertheless, Paul is not about to break the law in reference to slaves or anything else. There are Christians today, fed up with what they see as encroaching tyranny by the government, who are advocating various violations of the law. That is a sad commentary on their exegesis of the Scriptures. Christians, with the apostles, may say "We must obey God rather than men" only when the state clearly requires them to break a plain commandment of God. God gave authority to the home, to the church, to business and to the state. That authority must be fully respected by the Christian, even when it is wrongly used in many cases. It is only when the Christian himself is required by the state to sin that he demurs. He recognizes that it is the authority of God in each of these four areas that requires submission, but he sees that authority as limited, not absolute. So, like the three Hebrew officials in Babylon, he refuses to obey when asked to bow down to some purely human god (whether it be in the gross form of a physical idol, or in an idolatrous law enacted by the state). It is not a matter of how poorly the state uses his tax money that triggers his disobedience; the state, and those in power will have to answer to God for that. It is always the demand that a Christian engage in an activity that is sin that does so.

Today, many counselees have been wrongly influenced by movements that do not think as biblically as they should about such matters. At

13 I wanted to keep him with me that he might serve me in the bonds of the gospel on behalf of you.

---

best they are confused. You, as their guide through confusion, must have your own thinking in tact so as not to add to their confusion. You must be able to set forth a biblical rationale for what you say with clarity and conviction. The modern counselor will find himself faced with all sorts of ethical questions that he must have thought through ahead of time. That Paul is thinking of the legal implications of Onesimus' behavior, seems evident. The word that he uses can mean "to send back" or "to refer a case" for decision. Even if he uses the word in the former sense, something of the connotations of the latter would adhere to it. The adjudication of the case would be left up to Philemon; he alone had the right to make any decisions. But Paul, throughout the letter is playing the part of the defense attorney, pleading the case for Onesimus—*and* for himself. The latter fact, that Philemon must make a decision with reference, not only to Onesimus, but with reference to Paul as well, greatly strengthens the defense.

So, Paul is sending Onesimus back to Philemon, probably bearing this letter. It would be hard for Onesimus to return, but that was part of the evidence of the validity of his conversion. His return to face the music would be reason for Philemon to see fruit that was worthy of repentance. Often you will find it necessary to ask counselees to do hard things; including going back to those they have wronged. But notice, Paul does all he can to buttress Onesimus about as he returns. As he indicates, he is not merely sending him; along with him (by doing so) he is sending his own **heart (treat him as you would treat me)**. The appeal continues. Hardly a statement is made that is not couched in language calculated to touch Philemon's soul. To send back Onesimus is like tearing his own heart out and sending it! He explains: Onesimus has been such a help to me here in prison that I would like to have kept him here to continue to serve me. What you couldn't do for me (things that I know you would do if you were here and had the opportunity) he could do **on behalf of you**. But, I could not presume on you. You must tell me that you want to free him and send him back here to work with me in the gospel. Otherwise, you would have no occasion for exercising good-heartedness on your own. What you would do would be done out of necessity, not voluntarily.

It is often the part of the counselor to take a little extra time to achieve what he knows could be achieved simply by commanding it, in

14 Yet without your consent I didn't want to do anything, so that your goodness might not arise out of necessity but voluntarily.

15 Perhaps, then, this is why he left you for an hour—that you might have him back forever,

---

order to allow the counselee to come to the decision himself. While it is wrong to assume that he has all the information prepackaged within (Rogerianism), and will therefore, make a good decision if only given time, having given him adequate biblical information to make such a decision on his own (biblical counseling), you may often safely leave him to make up his own mind. When he does, not only does he do so voluntarily, as Paul indicates, but having made his own decision in the right way he will be strengthened by it. But, be sure that always, when you do this, the counselee not only has all the facts needed for good decision-making, but by your appeals, etc., you have prepared him for the right decision. That means that before turning the decision over to him, you ought to be as sure as Paul is here of the decision he will make. As the lawyer says, "I ask no questions of a witness to which I do not already know the answer."

Now, in verse 15, Paul says something quite remarkable: commenting on the providential working of God, he suggests, "perhaps...this is why he left you for an hour—that you might have him back forever." That is clear enough. In a nice comparison, he speaks of the evil behavior of Onesimus as temporary ("an hour") only, in God's providence, to bring about a permanent relationship on a holy and higher level: not that of slave to master, but brother to dear brother (there is that term again!). But what is remarkable in that?

The remarkable thing is that an apostle himself speaks of the providence of God in the way that he did. How often do we hear counselees and unthinking Christians of every sort speaking quite differently! They do not talk in terms of conjecture or suggestion ("perhaps"), but as if they had direct revelation about God's providential workings: "I know that this is what God wants me to do," and language of the sort is heard frequently in counseling rooms. How do they know? We are not talking about decisions based on explicit principles ("Thou shalt not commit adultery") but on matters that require judgments based on the application of general principles to specific, everyday affairs. Even Paul, who had seen God at work many times bringing permanent good out of temporary evil will not go that far: he says "perhaps." This passage, therefore, is an important arrow for the counselor to carry at all times in his quiver. It will help him

16 no longer as a slave, but more than a slave, as a dear brother (especially to me, but how much more to you) both in the flesh and in the Lord.

17 So then, if I am your partner, receive him as you would me.

18 If he wronged you in any way, or owes you something, charge that to my account.

---

immeasurably to keep counselees from running off halfcocked in various directions that would only lead to disaster. Because, even an apostle, who from time to time *did* receive direct revelation, apart from one, would not affirm with absolute certainty what God was doing prior to the fact itself, you can strongly make the point that the counselee ought not do so.

Onesimus, Paul assures Philemon, has become his dear brother, and he is sure that because of Philemon's relationship to Onesimus, his conversion would be even more precious to Philemon (v. 16). The new relationship that Onesimus now sustains to Philemon will be evident both in physical and in spiritual ways. So, since these things are true, Paul concludes, "if you count me as a partner in the work of the Lord, receive Onesimus **as you would receive me**."

Since Onesimus now meant so much to Paul (and should mean so much more to Philemon,) there was every reason to receive him as a joint partner in the work of the Lord. Paul has covered all the bases. He goes to lengths to be sure about every issue. He has thought through what he is going to say before he says it. Counselors need to take more time to be sure that they do the same. Not only do they often leave loopholes through which they allow the counselee to slither out of his responsibilities, but, by failing to cover the bases, they exert something less than the full pressure that needs to be brought to bear on him. Paul's pressure on his friend Philemon is relentless. Yet, it is kindly. It is tactful. But it is exerted in full force. That is the kind of counseling that is needed.

Speaking of covering the bases, Paul remembers one other item he wants to be sure to mention: if Onesimus, in leaving, caused financial loss to Philemon in some way, Paul wants him to know that he will stand by him: "You can charge that to my account," he magnanimously says. And, there are times when the counselor will take it on the chin for the counselee. There are times when he will reach into his wallet and give a counselee money to feed his family while exhorting him to find a job. Counseling must never become so impersonal that such things could not happen. I am not implying that you should ordinarily stand losses for you counselees; more often than not, that would do them harm. But there are

19 I Paul write this with my own hand; I will make restitution. (I'm not mentioning the fact that you owe me even your very self.)
20 Yes, brother, I need some help from you in the Lord; revive my heart in Christ!
21 I write to you, confident of your obedience, knowing that you will do even more than I have suggested.

---

situations in which you wonder whether or not you should. It is almost always wise to err, if need be, on the side of generosity. This statement by Paul not only assured Philemon, it also must have assured Onesimus of the genuineness of the apostle's love and backing. Gestures on your part toward the counselee (not always financial in nature. You might write letters of recommendation, etc.) also have the same effect.

Because of his problem in seeing (alluded to elsewhere), Paul often dictated his letters to an amanuensis. But he wants Philemon to know at least verse 18, if not the entire letter, is written by his own hand. That was a way of authenticating what was said. "You can hold me to this," Philemon, he is saying. "You have it in my own, unmistakable large letters." Again, he affirms **I will repay it**.

Then, he adds one more appeal: I'm not making a point of the fact, but, Philemon, you owe your own salvation to me. Both Onesimus and you are my converts; you both have the same spiritual father in the Lord. Perhaps this was the most powerful appeal of all, that Paul saved for the end as the clincher! Then, comes the outright request: "brother," (need I mention again the repeated use of the term,?) "I need your help. Please gladden my heart in Christ by agreeing to my request." It is the cry of one in need. And, do it for Christ's sake. (v. 20).

Paul now indicates that all his pleading and appealing is really something that he is telling Philemon to do: I am confident of your **obedience**. You will take my suggestions, I know, and treat them with the respect you would give to a command. I am confident you will do what I have requested—and even more! There is no hesitancy on the part of Paul to make large requests of God's people in the work of the Lord. What he requests for himself is, of course, not really for him; it is to enable him to carry on his work of evangelism. It is to further the honor and glory of Christ. Knowing Paul, Philemon would take all he said in that light. But, would your counselee? Only if he senses the same commitment to the Lord that was apparent to people who came into contact with Paul. For a man like Paul, a brother in Christ like Philemon would do almost any-

22   At the same time get a room ready for me, because I hope that through your prayers I shall be given to you.

   23   Epaphras, my fellow prisoner in Christ Jesus, greets you,

24   along with Mark, Aristarchus, Demas, and Luke, my co-workers.

   25   May help from the Lord Jesus Christ be with your spirit.

---

thing. Of that Paul was sure (v. 21). Be sure you sustain such a relationship to a counselee before exerting such pressures on him!

Paul was expecting to be freed from prison. When he was, he would visit Philemon. Was this also a means of putting pressure on him? Perhaps, but it was also a sincere request for Philemon to prepare a room. He hoped, as the result of the prayers of Philemon and others (cf. Philippians 1:25,26) to be set free (v. 22). Indirectly, this also was a request for continued prayer. The word "hope," used here, is not like our "hope-so" hope. Rather, it means "expectation" or "anticipation" based on solid grounds. Paul must have had some intimation of his coming release. Perhaps he received word through one of those who had become "saints in Caesar's household." We don't really know. But he seems fairly well-assured of the possibility.

According to verse 23, Paul was not alone in prison; Epaphras, about whom we learn much in the book of Philippians, was also imprisoned. He too sends greetings. And, then the others who were in and around the prison in Rome: Mark, Aristarchus, Demas (who, at this time was still with him) and Luke (co-workers with Paul) all send their greetings too. The fellowship of the saints is continually maintained and furthered by the allusion to individual names in Paul's letters. Here, they also serve as witnesses to what Paul writes and (in the future) to the response forthcoming by Philemon. They are with me, they concur with me, they too urge you to grant my request and they will all be waiting to hear how you will respond.

CONCLUSION

This brief, but rich letter, proportionately contains as much for the serious biblical counselor as larger, more prominent ones might. Do not forget or neglect it. When thinking of your own approach to others in counseling, read it again and again to learn tact. Read it to learn how to apply pressure on another inoffensively. From it learn how to make an appeal appealingly. Turn to verse 15 whenever you have to caution a counselee about presuming on the providence of God. Remember always to advise counselees to obey the law, even when it is difficult. Keep these, and other important factors we have mentioned in mind. It is truly a counselor's book.